A **Better Homes & Gardens** Book

An Imprint of

△◁▽○
HMH
www.hmhco.com

Better Homes & Gardens

DECORATING
BOOK

A HAPPY BLEND OF COLONIAL STYLING AND CONTEMPORARY COMFORT

Old and new— a happy blend

No matter how luxurious your home, or how simple; how gadabout your pattern of living, or how sedentary; how varied your tastes—it's easy to plan colors and furnishings that fit your family's living pattern.

If you lean toward the friendly warmth of Early American, but also

MAKES THIS FAMILY ROOM A FAVORITE GATHERING SPOT

like contemporary simplicity, consider the room above. Lighting, the sweeping drapery treatment, the entertainment center, all are boldly modern, tuned to maximum comfort.

Big accessories, massed plants, the picture grouping . . . these are in keeping with the contemporary architecture. Yet the personality, the flavor of the room is traditional.

It is achieved through Colonial furniture styles, scaled to fit today's homes; through small, allover pattern, subtle color and painted accent pieces; and through the knowledgeable use of accessories.

4

Contents

Dear Homemaker:

Everyone would like to live in a lovely and spacious home,
but until circumstance and fortune make it possible to do,
most of us must rely on our ability to decorate and arrange
our present home tastefully and comfortably so that it meets
our family's needs.

The new Better Homes & Gardens Decorating Book can
help you plan a home that comes nearest to your hopes and
means. Each chapter of the book approaches in a personal
and practical way one of the many problems confronted in
everyday decorating. The text speaks simply, and the illustratiions
say so much that you will be able to find your own solution
to these problems.

This is a book that both the layman and the student can
refer to with confidence; it has complete information to
make every home functional and individual, personally
satisfying, and beautiful.

Your home should have more than a pleasant appearance.
It should have a pleasant feeling, too . . . a feeling of welcome,
of family warmth, of comfort and convenience. Once you
understand the nature of color, space, and design stressed in
this book, your home will reflect good planning and radiate
a personality only you can give it.

We were fortunate and happy when Mrs. Jo Bull agreed
to work with Home Furnishings Editors and Book Editors in
developing and writing this Decorating Book.

Our pleasant association with Mrs. Bull spans several
years. Our respect for her practiced judgment and for her
professional frankness and understanding grows ever deeper.
Years of observing, reporting, and editing home furnishings
material have made her a realist about decorating.

We gratefully acknowledge our debt to the many regional
editorial assistants we call our scouts and to the several
photographers who have caught in verity the originality and
innovation of the best decorators over the entire country.

The Editors

Better Homes & Gardens

chapter 1

It's your home
what kind do you want?

These twelve pages will help you find the

decorating pattern that suits your family's

tastes . . . formal or casual . . . traditional,

Colonial or contemporary . . . simple or elegant

Pages **7** through **18**

Decorate to your way of living

Colonial settings
reflect cozy charm

Combine subtle colors
for an elegant feeling

Use easy-care materials
for informal living

Pastels and ruffles set
a sentimental mood

A formal home reflects
an orderly way of life

Decorate the
way you live

Do you entertain formally—or concentrate on back-yard barbecues? Do you have occasional help, or must your home be geared to easy care? Plan your decorating to further *your* way of living, to give you a comfortable, beautiful background.

What's your family's personality?

Good decorating takes into consideration the needs of everyone in the family. First step in planning your home is to provide for each facet of your family's composite personality.

Does your husband have "homework" to do—salesmen's reports, or after-hours figuring? Add a desk where he can work undisturbed.

Or perhaps your husband has a quiet hobby. Set aside a table in the living room where he can work and still enjoy your company. If one child is a mechanic junior grade, another a budding musician, reserve a place for each to work and play without annoying the other.

Consider not only the special needs, but also the everyday "musts" . . . "boy-proof" space with gay but sturdy furnishings, for small-fry playtime; a corner for knitting or sewing; a quiet spot to rest after a tough day.

Then work at making each of these places attractive and comfortable.

The whole family can give this room a real workout

All the ingredients necessary for mixing up a good party or a quiet evening of family fun are incorporated here.

Main area is perfect for dancing (rug rolls up) and games. Furniture is light, easily shifted. At the other end of the room is a small kitchen area for fixing snacks, and a piano.

If you're a bit sentimental—plan a cozy room

These homeowners planned their living room as a restful spot for reading and quiet conversation. The furniture grouping around the fireplace sets the welcoming spirit of the entire room.

Everything is designed for comfort—big tables, easily reached, tall lamps that fan out light for reading and give a rosy glow for beauty.

The color scheme stems from the flowered pattern of the draperies and quilted upholstery. The soft green on floor and walls is a perfect foil for deep rose and pink. The stately mantel is emphasized with white, repeated in the background of the drapery fabric. Black table top and graceful lamp bases underscore the brighter colors.

Treasured keepsakes—a handsome painting, fine china, and an antique chess set—add the final enrichment to the distinctive valentine color scheme.

Do you like old styles—or new?

Once you have established your family's preference for either a formal or casual setting, and have decided on the specific things you want your home to do for you, go ahead with planning your decorating scheme.

Do the gracious lines of time-tested Traditional furnishings especially appeal to you? Or do you prefer the sleek, dramatic look of Contemporary? And what about color—are the subtle colors your favorites, or do you like the vivid hues? Make your decorating decision—and then stick faithfully to it.

Look to Contemporary

Designed for formal living in a contemporary manner, this room has a feeling of space, furthered by simply styled furnishings.

Airy drapery fabric runs unbroken from wall to wall, ceiling to floor, makes ceilings look higher. Furniture gives room weight.

Prefer formal —or informal?

Your choice of furnishings styles should reflect your family's interests and living pattern

←*Traditional dignity*

Warm and serene, this traditional room reflects a composed and well-ordered living pattern. Brown tones range from soft beige to the honey of wall paneling, vibrant red-brown of tables and chair frames.

Colonial charm mirrors informal living

Red, white, and blue is the color theme here—framing a collection of treasured American antiques, reflecting a sense of cherished history. The sharp contrast of woodwork and walls is softened by taffy-toned pine and maple, sparked again with spirited red geraniums.

Furniture is cozily arranged to take full advantage of the hooded hearth on winter nights, for friendly conversations, or for larger parties. Desk chair and big wing chair are out of the traffic path through the door next to the fireplace, can move toward the center of the room for larger groups, without disturbing the more intimate arrangement.

The cupboard-desk between the windows ties them together in one unit.

The past can blend with
contemporary furnishings

Yes, the old and the new, the ornate and the simple, *can* be joined in a charming setting. The test is not in matching styles or periods, but in matching formality or informality. Here, a contemporary flowered rug is completely at home with shutters, antique pine table, modern Italian coffee table, ceramic bowl, and the stark lines of a simple chair. A carved eagle and modern painting make a dramatic decoration. This combination of old and new gives the room a homelike quality.

Sparkling color defines a gay, informal spirit

Who could be glum in a cheerful room like this? Vibrant carpet makes the brilliant floral sofa pattern in rose-red and shades of pink, accented with splashes of yellow, more vivid. The white walls and draperies, light paneling bordered by white brick, keep the strong color from being overpowering, and help to create an impression of space.

A traditional decor sets the mood for gracious living $\longrightarrow$

The grace and dignity of another day serve modern needs for comfort, take on new beauty with fresh colors. Here, the inside back of an antique mahogany desk is painted a pale ivory to silhouette a collection of lusterware. The same ivory appears in the background of chintz draperies and upholstery. Rug, walls, and lamp base are a light spruce blue.

Are you a busy clubwoman—with an active family? Then you'll want to decorate your home for a minimum of housework. Here, paneled walls and woven blinds need only occasional dusting. Textured rug, upholstery belittle dirt, are easy to clean.

Or are you a homebody—with a fondness for snug comfort? Soft seats are an invitation to conversation, with friends gathered 'round the hospitable fire. A brown and white print, accented by pink, inspires the room's handsome color scheme.

chapter 2

You know more
facts about color
than you think

Would you wear a checked blouse with a plaid

skirt? Would you choose a red dress to make

you look smaller? It's easy to use the color

facts you already know in decorating your home

Color is fun and easy to use

Contrasting colors emphasize

Make the most of handsome architectural features, point up the beauty of a prized chair or sofa, or create an exciting focal point of interest in your room. Colors that contrast boldly and sharply with background will make these features stand out, draw attention to them

Closely blended colors conceal

Want to hide an ugly radiator—or a monstrosity of a fireplace mantel—or the bulky lines of an awkward-looking but comfortable chair? Color them to blend with the wall behind, and they will be hardly noticeable. They will seem to melt out of sight before your eyes

Pale colors recede

The eye accepts pale colors without shock. These tones do not stop the eye, but let it seemingly look past and through. So use pastels and pale tints to make a room look larger. If ceilings are too low, white or light tones will give the room an impression of extra height

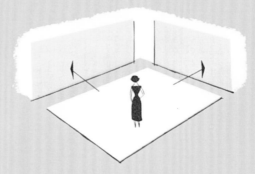

Bold colors advance

Bright, strong colors *do* stop the eye, give a feeling of coming toward you. They are good to use on extremely high ceilings, to bring them down into proportion with the furniture. Or square a long and narrow room by painting the end walls a brighter, bolder color

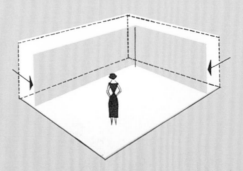

Color's an exciting tool

Bold colors advance pale colors retreat

Bold colors give an eye-fooling impression of bringing things closer — ideal to use in very large rooms, on high ceilings.

Use the pale and pastel colors to make a room look larger, lighter.

They're very effective if the room is too small or too dark — make the walls seem to stretch out into the distance.

Closely blended colors conceal

If you want to disguise an architectural feature, or hide bulky lines of a chair, blend it to the background with matching or similar color.

If you want to accent something, take a tip from the club lady in red. See how *she* stands out against that dull background. Make your fireplace or a lovely sofa the center of interest with color in contrast to the walls.

One bold pattern is usually enough

Too many cooks spoil the broth, and too many patterns spoil the room. Use restraint when choosing patterns. You probably wouldn't go out dressed like the golfer at the right— with his loud checked slacks, louder shirt, and even a plaid golf bag! Decorate your home in the same good taste you use when choosing your clothes.

If you've fallen in love with a definite pattern in bold design and color, use it dramatically. You can let it be the basis of your color scheme for the whole room. Select from it the other colors, for walls, carpet, and upholstery. Vary these with dull or bright finishes, textured or smooth weaves. You *can* use more than one pattern in a room if one is very simple, and complements the bolder. An indefinite stripe will always go well with either a floral or a geometric pattern and will not cause confusion of pattern.

Some colors are cool, some are warm

Coolness is suggested by blues and greens, the colors of water and trees. Use them in sunny rooms and on hot-weather porches. These are also the shivery colors of ice and snow, and will seem cold and dreary unless warmed with cheery accents, accessories.

Warmth is suggested by red, orange, yellow—the friendly colors of sunshine and glowing hearth. Sunless rooms welcome these. In concentrated form they recall the savage fury of desert sun and uncontrolled fire. Use these in small quantities for drama.

Unequal areas are more pleasing

Remember the dress hip line of the 1920s where the skirt and blouse were of equal length? It wasn't very flattering, partly because it wasn't pleasing to the eye. Today's fashions take this into account. In your own rooms, too, unequal color areas are more pleasing to the eye.

If your room were to be divided equally between two colors, you'd find a sharp division between the halves, instead of the organized, blended background you want. Select your major color to cover about two-thirds of the room's area. This will include at least part of the floor, the walls, the ceiling, the major surfaces.

Spark this major color with others for accent.

Color is affected by its neighbors

Keep this color fact in mind when you choose accessories and other room accents. Notice how the principle works here. The rust-brown scarf seems dull with the orange costume, becomes more colorful with black, is a bright accent worn with the green suit.

Give your rooms an entirely new atmosphere by shifting color emphasis in accordance with this principle.

If you've a red sofa that stands out against a blue rug, and red bookshelves against white walls, slip-cover the sofa to match the rug, and paint the bookshelves the same color. The room will look larger with this unbroken area of blue at floor level, with the shelves completing the scheme.

Put color to work for you

Furniture inspires color scheme

Carpet repeats the taffy tone of wood in the dining-room table and the chair frames.

One large area of color is often overlooked when making your decorating plans. The tones of the wood in tables, exposed chair frames, paneling, are just as important a part of the color scheme as carpets, paints, wallpapers, and fabrics. Plan these wood tones as part of scheme.

→

Choose from the taffy tones of pine and maple, grayed modern finishes, handsome mahogany — or brightly painted pieces for accent. If you want some pieces to match exactly, buy them together.

Reserve brighter colors for accents and accessories

Here bright red was used only on the lower half of wall, toned down with white above.

Bold colors advance—and in large quantities in a room they tend to close the walls in, sometimes even make them seem to lean forward, tilt out of line. You'll probably be happier and more comfortable, if you choose background colors that are a little subdued and more grayed.

→

Our friends here are unhappy. The small swatch looked like just what they wanted. On the walls it seemed to jump out at them. It's a good idea to get a big swatch of the color you plan to use. Fasten it to wall for effect.

Consider wood colors when you decorate

Large areas of color are more intense

The color wheel— a technical way to color success

A color wheel is the simple showing of the relationships of colors to each other. The experts who create colorful patterns in rugs, wallpapers and fabrics have planned from the wheel in a scientific manner. If we begin our schemes with one of these patterns, this research has already been

cool

These colors are dominated by blue. Like sky and water, they are cooling and restful

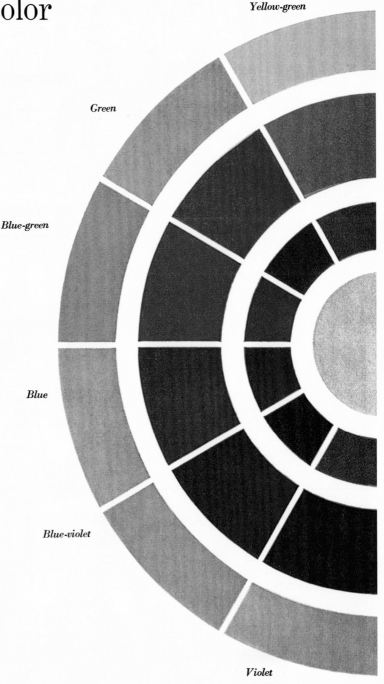

Yellow-green

Green

Blue-green

Blue

Blue-violet

Violet

done for us, and our decorating will be pleasing and beautiful.

There are three basic types of color schemes. The *monochromatic* uses tints, shades, and grayed tones of a single color—as, brown, beige, cream. The *analogous* combines colors that are side by side for a related scheme —as, green, blue-green, yellow-green. The *complementary* uses a pair of colors that are directly opposite—as, blue-green and red-orange.

Tone means the intensity of a color. *Value* refers to its lightness or darkness. Dark values are called *shades*. Light values are *tints*.

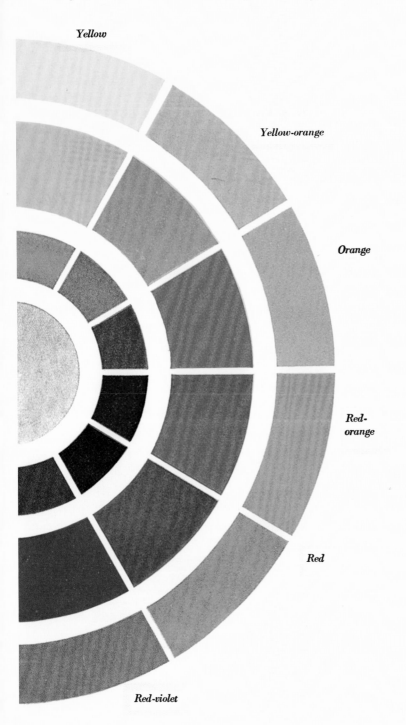

Yellow

Yellow-orange

Orange

Red-orange

Red

Red-violet

warm

These colors are dominated by red and yellow. Like fire, they are stimulating and exciting

Apply these rules to your home

You do know more about color than you think. The same principles you use to co-ordinate dress, shoes, hat, gloves, and accessories are easy and fun to apply to color in your home. Don't be afraid to use color—as a home decorator, it's your best friend.

Bold colors advance—seem to bring objects closer to you.

Pale colors recede—make a room look larger and lighter.

One definite pattern is enough—don't confuse a straightforward color plan with a jumble of design.

Some colors are cool—the colors in the half of the color wheel on page 24. Use these in a too-sunny room— you've a wide choice for any taste.

Some colors are warm—the colors in the half of the color wheel on page 25. Cheer up dull, cold rooms with any one of these warm tones.

Unequal areas of color are more pleasing—plan about two-thirds of your room in one color to be safe.

Color is affected by its neighbors—a white lamp blends into a pale beige wall. Against black it is dramatic. Used with a medium value, it both brightens and blends.

Wood is a color, too—consider the tones of wood pieces as part of your decorating scheme.

Large areas of color are more intense— subtle shades are your best choice for background areas.

Now, let's add one more good rule for decorating your home. A little poem will help you remember the elements of most well-decorated rooms. Be sure to include *something dark; something light, something dull; something bright*. The room above meets all these qualifications.

Color principles combine

in a well-decorated room

Pale, but warm, tones were used to make the room more cheerful, seem larger, lighter. One bold pattern distinguishes the fine sofa lines. The largest color areas are variations of brown—beige, cream, cocoa. Intense yellow is confined to small areas of chair seats and curtain stripes. Wood tones blend with the prevailing browns. The sofa and lounge chair frame are *dark*, the balance of the room *light*. Carpet and upholstery fabrics are *dull*, brass accessories are *bright*.

Pale colors recede

Pale and pastel colors visually expand the limits of a room—make the walls seem to fade into the distance, the ceiling look higher. And because pale colors reflect light instead of absorb it, these pale tones take full advantage of natural light, make artificial light more effective in the room.

Light colors are airy and open—ideal for the smaller rooms and open planning in so many new homes. But, although they are often used with contemporary furniture, they also help to create a cheery feeling of sunlight in dark, older homes.

If the major color areas in your room are light, include dark tones in some of the upholstered pieces and in accents. They'll add weight to the color scheme, keep the room from appearing to "float" away.

Pale colorings put a special emphasis on textures and patterns—even the shadows cast on a light wall can become part of the decorating plan.

Cool or warm

Light colors can be either cool or warm, depending on which side of the color wheel they stem from. Pale blues and greens give a fresh look to a sunny room, while creamy yellow or pink cheer a cold room.

White works visual magic

White background opens up this contemporary room, gives a feeling of spaciousness. Delicate as this scheme is, it's still practical for families with young children. Hard-surfaced flooring, painted walls, washable fabrics, are easy-care factors.

See how much closer this boldly colored wall seems than the pale one next to it. This cheerful, stimulating hobby pattern domi-nates the breakfast area, but is tempered by the adjoining, pale wall. Clear, strong yellow adds an extra color boost to the area.

Bold colors advance

Bold, bright colors give an impression of bringing things closer—and help create decorating magic in your home through their imaginative use.

By painting one wall a bold tone, the other three in a pastel of the same color, you'll change the shape of a square, boxy room. The bright wall will seem to come toward you, the pale walls will seem to recede.

Use the same principle to square up a long, narrow room, by painting the short walls in bold color, the long walls in a neighboring pastel.

Make the most of handsome architectural features with the bright treatment, too. They'll catch your eye from any place in the room.

Bold colors are friendly

Everyone has two subconscious and conflicting desires. One, to be free and unconfined; the other, to be warm and friendly and together with a group. Bright, bold colors used as accents and accessories help relate the people in a room to the room itself. Used with large areas of pale colors, both needs are satisfied.

Features here are the handsome fireplace and the picture window. Both were given bright color to emphasize them, visually draw them closer together. When the draperies are open, the green fireplace and chaise longue frame the view.

WHITE FIREPLACE AND TRIM EMPHASIZE THE ARCHITECTURAL DETAILS

Sharply contrasting colors
emphasize your furnishings

BRIGHT ROSE-RED AND PINK, WITH WHITE ACCENTS, DEFINE THE FURNITURE

If you have a flair for the dramatic, like the stimulation of bright color, want to show off your fine furnishings . . . then you will probably be happy with a sharply contrasting color scheme in your home.

If the room you are decorating needs variety, a contrasting scheme will give you the desired effect, without introducing definite pattern or texture. It will clearly define each separate piece of furniture, while all the architecturally interesting points will stand out sharply.

Closely blended colors conceal

If you are warm and friendly, like a restful, comfortable atmosphere about you . . . then you will probably enjoy a blended color plan. This is a color scheme where all the colors are related to one another, so that the eye moves smoothly without the distraction of sharp contrast, emphasizing a way of living, rather than furnishings.

If the architectural details in your room are too ornate for your tastes, or if the room is cut up, or small, conceal these defects by painting walls and woodwork the same color, with a lighter, blending, shade for the ceiling. Choose blending wood tones for your furniture, too, and upholstery fabrics in plain or print that carry colors closely related to the background shades.

Chairs of different shapes and sizes will look as though they belong together if they are slip-covered or upholstered in an identical pattern.

One pattern, one major color, give a feeling of unity

Ornate fireplace, walls, and window are united with paint and matching draperies. Fabric pattern blends, too, as do the warm wood tones of the furniture. Accents of gold and blue are carefully repeated in candle sconces, table and break-front accessories. Note how one pattern is repeated in entrance hall.

Select one definite pattern then repeat it

A bold print in matching paper and fabric sets the theme here

This color scheme begins with the warm patchwork design of the hall paper and the matching living room slip covers and draperies. Grayed-green woodwork stems from the pattern, and a brighter tone is in the carpet. Tiny blue note is picked up as the only accent color.

Choose one definite pattern, and repeat it—that's the secret of decorating with pattern. The one pattern could be in a rug, a wall covering, or the draperies, with the other colors in the room taken from it. If you introduce more than one definite pattern, they will fight with each other for attention and lose importance.

Select a tone from the design, for your backgrounds—floor, ceiling, or walls, depending on where the pattern is used. Then pick a bright color from the pattern, and use it throughout the room as an accent, in lamps, pillows, ash trays, or other accessories.

This big, bright pattern is calmed with a neutral background

Reflecting the family's love of horses, a hobby print sets the pace in a recreation room. Beige tones in the pattern are reflected in honey-colored wood paneling. Bright red and green are the only accents. A collection of china horses helps carry out the room's theme.

Warmth is suggested by the colors of fire and earth

Oranges, yellows, reds, and the red-browns—these are the colors of sun, fire, earth, suggesting the friendliness of a campfire, the warmth of the sun, the natural "belonging" of rich soil and rock and sand.

Subtly, and almost without recognition on your part, these colors will give you the same comfortable feeling of warmth and friendliness.

Too much warmth, though, can be uncomfortable to live with. Large areas of warm colors should be confined to party rooms, or used in kitchens where dull chores need perking up.

If you love these bright colors, it's wise to contrast them with cool colors —blues, white, blue-greens. Or use these tones to emphasize and bring out the lines of one fine piece of furniture or an architectural detail.

Sun tones set the stage for entertaining friends

The warm earth tones in the flooring and rug, brilliant chair seats and pillows, massed dramatically against stark white with touches of black . . . these are the ingredients that make this an exciting, stimulating room for a party.

There's enough color to catch the eye without disturbing it.

Coolness comes with the tones of water, trees

Coolness is suggested by the colors of water and trees . . . the soft blue-greens of a young spruce, or spring grass . . . the subtle green-blues of lakes and ponds . . . the deep-water blue of the ocean . . . the sharp, light blue of shadowed ice and snow.

If you live in a hot climate, or if the room you are decorating is overwhelmed by the glare of the western sun, consider planning your color scheme around these cool colors.

Since these are nature's colors, they go well together, and they can be accented by a multitude of colors.

If your basic scheme is cool, vary it with smaller amounts of warm tone. Red, pink, yellow, yellow-greens, browns, and beiges—all of these will fit easily into a cool theme.

The intensity is important, too. Strong shades can emphasize the lines of your furnishings, while pale shades make them seem to disappear.

Blue, white, and green blend in a cool and comfortable room

The expanse of snowy white walls creates a cool feeling in this bedroom. Soft spring green and the blue of a summer sky in lamp and accessories enliven the scheme. Deeper blue, sharp black, underscore and emphasize the light tones. Pale golden yellow adds a necessary note of warmth to the room.

Even though green, blue, and white are essentially cool colors, there are variations in tone which can send them over to the warm side.

If you remember your school days, you'll remember that equal parts of primary blue and yellow combine to make a pure green. The more blue, the cooler the tone, the more yellow, the warmer the green gets.

Both aqua and turquoise combine blue and green, and, since there is a touch of yellow in the green, these colors are warmer in effect than a pure, primary blue would be.

Adding a drop or two of blue to white will make it even cooler, less dazzling than the pure color, and it will then blend into a blue room without too sharp a contrast. Conversely, adding a drop or two of beige or yellow will "antique," or warm it.

Cool as a spring night

Cool, bright blue is warmed with yellow-green

Two of the primary colors—blue and yellow—combine with white to form this color scheme. The third—red—is the bright accent.

Over two-thirds of the color area is in cool tones—the sweep of blue carpet, emphasized by sofa and stool—white walls and ceiling, white table tops, the panels, and the accessories.

The next largest areas are the warm yellow-green chairs and yellow-beige wood paneling and furniture finishes. All are sparked with the bright gold in the tables, and the stool.

A blue and green color scheme will blend and harmonize if you use some yellow tones to tie these two colors together. The yellow can appear in its primary state, for accent, or in yellow-green tones like lime or lemon —or in warm, yellow-beige finishes in paneling or furniture.

When you plan a cool color scheme, first decide on the large areas—carpet, walls, major upholstery pieces.

At least two-thirds of the total color area should be in cool tones. Then you can divide the remaining third into semi cool and warm colors, light and dark, bright and dull, to give proper balance to the room.

Just as in any other color scheme, subdued tones "live" best in large amounts, with medium values in such areas as sofas and chairs, and bright colors for sharp accents.

Beautiful color, well-planned furniture arrangement, and careful use of accessories create a memorable room

Unequal areas of color are more pleasing

The aim of your decorating is to blend the various elements of your room—in color, in furniture arrangement, in style—into one harmonious unit that will serve as a background for your family's activities.

When you plan your color scheme, let one color dominate. Unequal areas of color are more pleasing to the eye —in a dress, in a picture, or in a room. Exactly equal areas create a confusing division, separate one part of the room from another, and give equal emphasis to each part.

Well over half of your room should carry this dominant color, in one tone or another. It could vary from a deeply shaded carpet to a pale ceiling, with medium values in between. Spark it with bright accents. Be sure to repeat the accent color in varying amounts throughout the room.

Cool white is dominant here, still, the room glows with pleasing color and warmth

Five-sixths of this room is white—the walls and the ceiling. Here it serves to exploit and dramatize the brilliance of the upholstery fabric and accessories, the subtle blending of the carpet with the pale shutters.

The golden grouping near the fireplace calls attention to its hospitality. The quilted fabric is touched with blue and white.

Color is affected by its neighbors

Point up furnishings with contrasting color

In the room at the left, the homemaker wanted to emphasize the lines of a provincial sofa and camouflage the tall louvered screen.

So she painted the walls to blend with the screen, and to contrast with the sofa.

In the room below, the sofa color mingles with the lime-green walls. Now the screen becomes the decorating point of interest, sharply contrasting with the wall color, yet blending with the other wood tones of the furniture.

Green sofa stands out against beige, screen blends.

Green sofa blends into lime-green walls, while wood screen is emphasized.

Red sofa vividly contrasts with carpet, which blends with wall colors.

Change a background to contrast or blend colors

In the room above, the tweedy dark blue carpeting with a white thread in it, harmonizes with the dark wall colors and with the wood trim. The red sofa is a bright accent, repeated in flowers and a shelf section.

In the room at the right, a sharp red shifts the decorating emphasis to the floor by blending the sofa in as part of a major color area. Navy blue and white walls and woodwork are now in vivid contrast to the carpet.

Red is also repeated in curtains, flowers, shelf interior.

Now, sofa color melts into unbroken sweep of red.

Color is versatile

See what a difference just a change in color relationships can make. You can plan for contrast, harmony, or an exact matching of tones.

When you start your planning, give some thought to the way your colors will look together—the effect of one on the other. If your sofa is upholstered in gold, and you want to show off its lovely lines, put it against a contrasting wall, perhaps a bright blue-green, or some other color with very little yellow tone in it.

If you want to hide the sofa's bulk and proportions, put it against a wall of exactly the same shade.

If you want to blend it into the color scheme, but preserve its identity, place it against a color that has some gold tones in it—a lime, or yellow-beige—or against a pattern that has a gold motif in it, among others in the design.

When you redecorate, start with the colors you know you want to keep. Then, whether you are buying new slip covers—or new draperies—or rugs—or tables—consider the relationship of the colors you already have to those you are planning to add. Play them up, play them down, or blend them into your scheme.

Green curtains melt into a green wall

An all-of-a-color background erases the divisions between curtains, dado, and upper walls.

Matching the color makes this small dining room seem bigger, because the eye is not stopped or distracted. Curtains become part of large color area.

The curtains are a strong emphasis against the red wall

In this version of the dining room, the green curtains become a striking design against a contrasting wall. The plain dado, the patterned upper walls, and the curtains form a series of breaks that stop the eye, bring the walls in closer with a friendly, "homey" atmosphere.

Wood is a color

You've developed a color plan that contains all the elements of your room—paints and papers, slip cover, upholstery, and drapery fabrics, carpeting. But wait—there's a piece missing. *Wood is a color, too.*

Consider what a large part of your color area is in wood finishes—in the living room, in larger quantities in the dining room, and in bedrooms.

Select the colors of these woods just as you choose any other color for the room. First, establish the basic plan, around the things you must keep, or with the things you intend to buy, in mind. Then get down to specifics—the tones and shades to go in each place, on each piece.

Don't try to match all the woods in one room. The effect will be much more pleasing if the finishes and the woods themselves vary a little. They should blend with each other, however, and be consistent to the basic color scheme. And don't overlook the accent possibilities in one important, contrasting piece of furniture.

Soft honey tones of wood blend with background colors

Here, a variety of woods in the cabinet, tables, and floor blend well together in a handsome Early American room.

All are part of the basic brown-beige scheme, yet the differences add variety and interest within the scheme. Blue upholstery and lamp base, fresh white curtains temper the warmth.

Fireplace wall in strong

color accents a quiet room

Dramatic orange of sofa upholstery and the fireplace wall is limited and emphasized by the basic color scheme of white, gray and charcoal. If curtains were orange, too, effect would be too bright for comfort.

Color
in quantity
becomes
intense

If you plan to use a bright color in large areas, such as on your walls, or on the floor, do try to see a man-size swatch of it before you actually apply it. You will generally find that the sharpness should be cut down a little, or grayed.

A little bit of bright color may look alluring, but on your walls, it will just jump at you. The larger the amount, the more intense it will seem.

If most of your color area is subdued, then one bright wall will give the impression of a larger space than actually exists. A vivid floor covering accounts for one-sixth of the color area.

chapter 3

How to build a
color scheme

It's easy to plan a color scheme—follow a few

simple principles for professional-looking

results. Here are 68 color pictures that will

give you ideas and suggestions on how to do

Plan satisfying color proportions

Neutrals for large areas

You'll probably be more comfortable and "at home" with your color scheme if you select soft neutrals or grayed tones for the largest color areas in your room—the walls and the floor. The more subtle shades give a restful feeling. It's a good idea to hang a swatch of the color you've chosen on the wall, live with it a week to see if you like it

1. Use neutral tones for the walls and floor

Medium tones on furniture

Next to the six sides of the room —floor, walls, ceiling—your biggest color areas in the living room are the upholstered pieces, such as chairs and sofas. In the kitchen, it's counter tops; in the bedroom, it's the spread. You can make your room more inviting by using a medium tone in such places. Repeat shade in room for balance

2. Use medium tones of color on sofas, chairs

Use strong color sparingly

Reserve the really bold and bright tones for accessories and accent notes that will pep the room up, give you a spark of interest without too much excitement for day-to-day comfort. Pillows, ashtrays, bright mats for your pictures . . . the sharp colors of highly glazed ceramic accessories—these are the places for the strong, bright tones

3. Keep bright, strong colors as the accent note

Where you can look for
color schemes

Select a pattern you like — in drapery or upholstery fabric, in wallpaper, or on a dish. You can use these colors in decorating.

Find a picture or some other wall decoration that has several colors in it. Use these colors as the scheme for decorating your own rooms.

Pick your favorite color, and build decorating scheme around it. Keep it simple, use shades from bright to dark for interest, contrast.

Your garden in the springtime, the hues of a rose, a cherished memory of a vacation-time view — all can be a color scheme beginning.

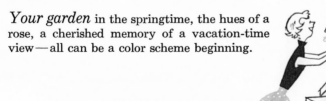

Choose from a carpet's jewel tones or smart pattern — the streaks in a linoleum — the multi-toned dots in a handsome vinyl tile square.

You can start your scheme with a wallpaper pattern

A transportation print sets the theme for a family room

Because the wallpaper pattern is so bold and colorful, it needs to be surrounded with more subtle tones. Color of the train smoke goes into walls and curtains. Carpeting repeats the bright red. Brown, beige are major upholstery colors.

There are three steps to a color scheme. First, the background colors, for floor, walls, and ceiling. Second, the next largest color areas—major upholstery pieces in the living room, the spread in the bedroom, the finish of your table in the dining room. Last come the intense accents.

The "something you like" may be a wallpaper pattern. First, select the floor color, then walls, trim, and the ceiling from it. You will like the latter better if they're subdued, to set off the other colors in the room.

Then choose the upholstery tones, and, finally, the accents. If you stick to the colors in the pattern, you will have a harmonious scheme.

Warm and cheerful air creates a comfortable family room

The colors are well distributed—each repeated several places in the room. Deep, cool blue accents the color plan. For an alternate scheme, you could use pale blue walls and curtains, deep blue carpeting, with sharp accents of yellow-red.

Pretty paper, companion fabric are starting point for scheme

Companion prints set the scene for a living-dining area

A sunny, flower-patterned paper is the choice for a dining area. From it are selected brown tones for other walls and the carpeting, smaller upholstery pieces.
The blue motif is subdued for sofa fabric. The accents are bright orange.

There are many wallpaper patterns and fabrics especially designed to be companions. Sometimes these match exactly. Often the background pattern of one is repeated in the other, without the bolder overpattern.

Select the basic color scheme from the smaller, allover pattern. First, choose muted background colors for walls, floor, and ceiling; then brighter ones for major upholstery pieces.

Look to the big pattern for the striking accents. However, limit these to two, or three, at the most.

Although separate, these areas are harmoniously planned

The dining area is separated from living space by its gay, flowered wallpaper, blended with it by draperies of the companion fabric. Another choice would be yellow walls, deep blue carpeting, brown sofa, orange lounge chair, accents.

Patterned fabric inspires well-balanced color plan

Living room color scheme comes from a flowered print

Coolness and dignity were the goal in this room. So shades of green were chosen for the carpeting and upholstery, deep blue for the sofa, blue-green for the walls, soft blue for small pieces. Rose-pink and red sparkle as the accents.

Beginning with any pleasing pattern is probably the easiest way to develop a harmonious color scheme, since all the elements you need are right in front of you. It is only a matter of deciding which color or colors to emphasize, which to use in smaller quantity, and which to eliminate.

If your pattern is a multicolored one, the biggest problem will be what to discard. Too many colors in a room are only confusing. Stick to three or four major colors at the most with some variation of tone within the colors, and you'll come out with a much more pleasing room scheme.

So be ruthless in your selection, and take plenty of time to be sure of your decision. First come the background colors, then the major upholstery pieces. Finally, take two or three bright tones for accents.

Cool greens and blues develop a restful atmosphere

Greens and blues, stemming from a bright floral print, supply the major color areas of floor, walls, and upholstery. An alternate scheme could have violet carpeting, purple and green upholstery, with accents of pale pink, blue and white.

FOR BALANCE, FABRIC PATTERN IS REPEATED IN A CHAIR ACROSS THE ROOM

Let the colors of the fabric pattern dominate the room

THE DARK GRAY IN THE FABRIC BLENDS WITH LIGHTER GRAY OF THE SOFA

The touch of white from the pattern is the wall tone, chosen to lighten a dark room, make it look bigger. Lamp bases and shades repeat the color. A softer shade of the fabric background is in the carpeting, and a still lighter shade on the sofa. While different in value, these three shades blend with one another, give variety within the same neutral background.

The two rose-red upholstered chairs and the black pillows supply the accent note. Both the rose-red and the black are found in the pattern.

Color stems from a patterned
floor covering

*Take a scheme from a many
colored hard-surface flooring*

A family room should be comfortable, practical, easy to clean—and handsome, too.

Meet all of these requirements by starting with a hard-surface floor, in an allover design that will not show footmarks or dust, and in a variety of colors that can set your decorating scheme.

In the room below, walls, draperies, wood tones, blend with the beige background of the tile. Green, coral, and yellow brighten the room, stem from the tile colors.

A decorative rug or carpet also keys a color plan

The same planning procedure followed with a wallpaper or fabric pattern can be used when you start your color scheme with a decorative rug or carpet.

First, select the background colors for walls and draperies. Then come the slip cover, upholstery, and wood tones. And finally, choose the bright accent and accessory colors.

In the room above, the wall tone blends with the rug border. Draperies combine this neutral shade with a stripe that matches the blue flower of the pattern. The sofa is upholstered in soft beige. Wood tones pick up the darker brown. The accent is soft blue.

Start with a
picture

The procedure for selecting a color scheme is the same—whether the pattern is found in a wallpaper print, a fabric, or a picture.

Think of the picture as a design—forget its subject matter and concentrate on its colors and their distribution and importance. The artist has

already decided on the colors to be emphasized, amounts to be used.

Study your picture . . . which are the greatest areas of color—should they be used on walls, flooring, draperies, upholstery—or on all of them, leaving the sharp accents only for the smaller pieces and for accessories?

The sophisticated color scheme above stems from the dramatic painting over the fireplace. Soft gray-browns are drawn from it for floor, drapery tones, for wood panel finish —spiked with sharp chocolate for small wall expanse. Ice-cream pastels, brighten chairs, pillows.

Plan your room around a
precious heirloom piece

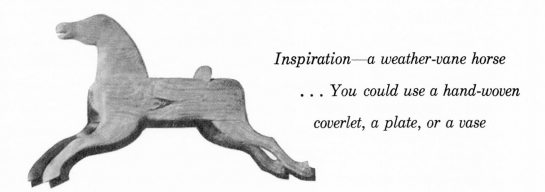

Inspiration—a weather-vane horse

. . . You could use a hand-woven

coverlet, a plate, or a vase

The "something you like," the item around which you want to build your color scheme, might be an antique or a cherished family heirloom.

The same procedure is followed as before—first the background, then the secondary colors in upholstery, slip covers and wood tones, then the sharper accents and accessories.

If the heirloom is patterned, your color scheme will fall into place with little trouble. Decide which colors to emphasize, which to use in small quantities, which to eliminate.

If the prized possession is all one tone, as in a simple vase of subtle green, use that shade as your starting point, and build around it.

Furniture styles need not be antique. They can be as contemporary as you wish, with just the colors stemming from your heirloom.

Warm wood tones create a pleasing background

The taffy tones of an antique weather vane blend with the pine paneling, the polished plank flooring, and the tawny chest—once an old dry sink.

Wood color is deepened and underscored with the dark rug border and the painted rocker, accented with gleaming copper, and red in the rug and sofa.

Adapt color from a lovely view

Brown, beige, green, and blue predominate in this mountain view. White snow, reddish rocks, almost black shadows are also vital color factors.

You can recreate your memories of the most beautiful view you've ever seen—transmute them into concrete, everyday surroundings.

Nature's colors are usually restful, pleasing to live with. Your only problem is how to go about arranging them. First, take a long and careful look at the slide or color snapshot of a favorite vacation scene.

In the picture above, brown tones, values of blue and green are predominant. The brown of the earth and far-away rocks was selected for the floor covering. To make the room seem bigger, the walls were painted a sky blue. A blue and black plaid carries two of the scene's colors, is dramatized by grass-green on the studio couch and bookcase.

Accents derive from view

Accent colors come from the scene, too. There's a touch of deep red in the rocks, applied to the room in the tole lamp. Colors of the white snow, beige rocks show in the wall map.

COLORS FROM FAVORITE VIEW ARE TRANSLATED INTO A STUDY SCHEME

The hot, sharp, reds and yellows and oranges of this mass of midsummer flowers are softened with pale pink and white blossoms, cooled by the filler of deep green foliage.

Color scheme stems from a
garden

Do you have memories of the most beautiful garden you've ever seen— of pale hyacinths and crocuses, of bright tulips or golden jonquils in the springtime—of flaming coxcomb or brilliant zinnias in the summer?

Perhaps you've walked through the fertile flamboyancy of the tropics, or a neat New England garden—or seen the sudden flowering of a desert cactus, or the delicate blossoms of azaleas in the Deep South.

Maybe your own garden is the one you love the most, from early lilacs to pale pink roses, to the riot of late chrysanthemums and dahlias.

You can re-create the loveliness of any one of these memories, to be permanently yours in your own home.

Build a color scheme around the garden you have loved the best.

You can start with the flowers themselves, or with a picture of the flowers you want to translate into color in your home. The picture is a little easier to work with—and it is certain to be there when you need it.

Learn to eliminate

Follow the regular process for your color scheme—select the background tones, then the secondary areas, then the accents. You will find the result more pleasing if you stick to just three or four colors. Eliminate all the other colors in your garden palette from the color scheme.

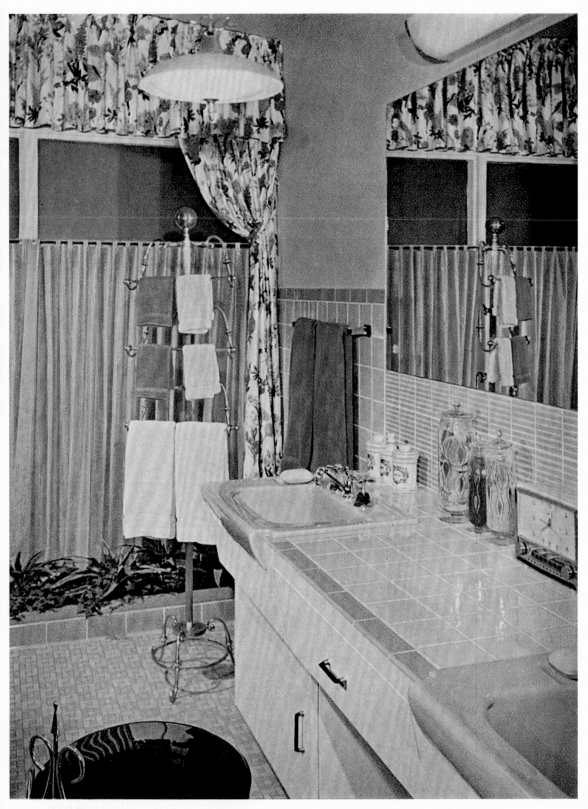

BATHROOM COLOR SCHEME STEMS FROM SUMMERTIME GARDEN COLORS

BLUE SHUTTERS, CUSHIONS, DINNERWARE, ARE THE STARTING POINT

If you start with your *favorite color*

You'll be able to find your favorite color in solid tones, or in patterns.

First, select a paint, a wallpaper, floor covering, fabric, or accessory in the shade which you decide to use. Then choose the rest of your furnishings to complement and blend with this dominant room color.

Blue accents neutral background

This color scheme began with the blue and white drapery fabric. White walls and gray carpeting emphasize the blue. Upholstery fabrics strengthen blue note, as do the accessories.

If your favorite color is

green

When you choose green as your favorite, you've selected an almost perfect color to enhance any other you may wish to use. Just as nature uses vast expanses of green to show off the myriad tones of blossoms, so can you use the greens to complement or contrast with any other colors.

It's a wise move, too, if you like the excitement of change. Because green "goes with" every other color, you can achieve quick variety by replacing accent and accessory colors . . . always with the assurance that the new color will look just right.

Cool off a too-bright room with a green that has a bit of blue in it—warm a cold room with a green that leans to the yellow. Whichever color direction you take will help give the effect of summertime warmth in winter, of grassy coolness in summer.

A variety of green tones dominates this subtle scheme

Ranging across the spectrum from yellow-green to sharp emerald, from pale walls to the deep shininess of leaves, the greens in this room blend into an elegant background for the sharp accents of gold, brass, and blue. Equally pleasing would be other accessory tones . . . reds and pinks, oranges or violets.

If your favorite color is
melon

The warm tones of melon—that between-orange-and-red color—are often preferred by outgoing people.

These are the exciting, tangy colors of sun and fire—and must be used with restraint, or the final result will be overpowering.

If the room you are planning faces north, or is dark, or will be used primarily as a party room, you can afford to be a little more bold with melon. Warm the room, perhaps, with a pale tone on the walls. Or use it at its sharpest and brightest on a painted chest, or in a pouf rug, or to dramatically outline a door.

If your room is already light and bright, reserve melon for the accents that give character, letting the walls and floor and upholstery carry duller, less exciting color. For happiest results, tone bright melon down.

Discreet use of vivid melon warms a distinguished room

One strong color is the secret of this room's charm—melon, used against the neutrals of light walls, polished woods.

Diversified in tone, the color is pointed up by concentrating it in one area of the room. From chair seat to lamp to the upholstered chair, it runs the gamut from pale to deep.

If your favorite color is pink

Pink is delicate and subtle, feminine and soft—and flattering to most everyone. It can be warm with the addition of a little yellow—leaning toward a peach tone. It can be cool with the addition of a little blue—leaning toward the violet. Because it is essentially a pastel, pink should be used with another stronger color, to point it up, bring out its pleasant tone. The second color can be bright or dark. Flame accents of the same value are particularly dramatic.

Pink blends well with grays and browns, sharp blues. Combined with purples and lavenders it is truly feminine and delightfully fresh.

Pink is a wonderful color to use in a party room. It suggests fun and gaiety.

←

Fragile and lovely—

pink in a bedroom

Pink gauze curtains, shirred and hooked to a traverse track, reach from floor to ceiling. Unlined, they show their greatest beauty with the sunlight shimmering through the folds. Venetian blinds hang behind, for privacy when needed.

Sharp red is the strong note that underscores the fragility of the pink scheme.

→

Variations of pink—

lovely against beige

Fresh, clear colors contribute to over-all effect. Strawberry pink Chippendale type sofa repeats pink in the raspberry and white floral upholstery on the modified Queen Anne chairs.

Variations of these colors are seen in the stripe covering the chair in the lower right, and on the sofa pillows.

If your favorite color is yellow

Yellow is sunny lift to black and white

A small dining room gets a new lift with a basic black-white color scheme brightened with golden yellow.

Color in the floor-to-ceiling draperies is repeated in new upholstery for the chair seats, unifies this combination of modern and traditional furnishings.

The bubble ceiling light repeats white of the walls and the table; brass blends with yellow tone. Geometric wallpaper, hard-surfaced flooring, shutters, express modern feeling.

Rich golds enhance traditional setting

A view window without a view becomes the decorating center of interest, with a dramatic sweep of drapery and the swag which has been used as a cornice.

The window treatment provides a background for sofa grouping looking toward a fireplace. A touch of brown turns bright yellow into these elegant gold tones, blends them with the carpet. Deeper brown of the chair frames and the coffee table give the "something dark" here.

If the quiet
brown
tones are
your favorites

Warm, comfortable, and earthy—
there is a solidity, a "hominess" about
the brown tones that make them
universal favorites. Ranging from the
palest of cream-beiges to the deepest
of black-browns, these tones can be
used together in a room to give infinite variety without dullness.

There are two basic kinds of brown
tones—those tinged with gray, those
touched with red. When you make
your first selection of the color you
want for upholstery, carpet or walls,
keep a swatch of it for reference when
you buy other things for the room.

You'll want to stay within the gray
or the reddish range, and they're
hard to select without a sample. Any
of the brown tones is essentially warm,
so choose cool accents.

A shell of reddish-browns is
cooled with white accents

The distinctive color of the paneled
walls and the sharp underscoring of
reddish tones in cushions combine to
make a handsome color scheme.

But, for real comfort, as well as
beauty, the room needs a cool touch.
Off-white chair and pillow, the lamp
and shade, offer the prime contrast.

Work with the brown tones

It isn't the colors you choose, but the way you use them, that makes a room gay or subtle, sophisticated or informal. One of the reasons for the popularity of the brown tones lies in their versatility—they'll blend into either casual or formal homes.

Brown is a good selection for use with natural-wood paneling, both in contemporary and traditional settings. The one-color background which displays pattern and design in its furnishings, requires a wide variety of texture and tone within the color, to avoid a monotonous feeling.

The use of warm tones of wood for backgrounds and for furnishings extends to these same tones in paints and papers, in rugs and carpets.

Subtle browns, taupes, beiges, ranging from deep chocolate to light cream and combined with natural-wood finishes, will give you this one-color look, but one that is rich and elegant. You won't go wrong if you use the darkest tones on the floor, the palest on the ceiling, and variations of the medium values in-between.

←

Blue touches enliven a brown scheme

Blue, taken from a finely scaled fabric in warm yellow-browns, highlighted by blue, green, and orange, covers a small side chair, reappears in carpeting. Rich wood paneling provides the mellow background color. Sofa is bright orange accent.

→

Subtle browns enlarge a contemporary room

All-of-a-color, with tones ranging from soft creamy-beige to deeper cocoa, this contemporary setting intermingles the textures of wood paneling and fabrics. Lacking a sharp break in color, the room visually appears more spacious.

Gray -a good background for Contemporary

Gray is essentially a cool color, and if it is your favorite, you probably like cool blues and greens, too, lots of room, and the feeling of space.

Gray, in its lighter tones, is an excellent background color to use for expanding the open-plan interiors of Contemporary architecture.

A pale gray will visually "push" the walls away. Used from room to room, ranging from very light to a medium value, it will give a neutral background to all furnishings.

If you like vivid contrasts, gray is a good background choice. Almost any other color looks more vibrant when used with gray. Bright tones glow, whites and blacks, especially, are starkly brilliant against gray.

Major color warms gray

If you want to blend in the background even more, warm the gray you're using with the other major color in the room. Possibly it's blue or red, brown or yellow—your choice depends, too, on your other colors.

In the handsome living room at the right, gray walls are shaded lightly with green to soften the tone, blend it with the green of the upholstery pieces. Brilliant flowers still stand out against the gray walls.

A SHELL OF GRAY ENCIRCLES

COOLNESS OF GREEN AND WHITE FURNITURE, SHARPENED WITH BLACK

Gray is also good with Traditional

Here is the other side of the story—cool gray elegantly translated into a distinctive traditional setting. This color scheme got its start with a pair of prized antique bowls, now displayed on the mantel.

Since the room has many windows and is very light, the soft, cool gray of the patterned border on the bowls was selected as the dominant color.

The drapery and upholstery fabric pattern has the same gray background, warmed by a golden-yellow flower, and touched with white.

The other major upholstery color is soft gold on the sofa and chair.

If the room had been very dark, the scheme could have been reversed, using sunlit gold as the dominant color, accented by the neutral gray.

The accessories keep to the yellow, gray, and white theme.

Dark, light, dull, bright

Remember the jingle of "something dark, something light, something dull, something bright"? Here, the background is dull, to absorb light, gives a pleasant, restful feeling. Mahogany tables and marble hearth are the "something dark."

Light gold is a major color, and the vivid yellow-gold of the bowls and the flower pattern provide bright accents. The luster of bowls, polished andirons, and woods, also adds "something bright."

GRAY IS WARMED WITH YELLOW, IS

UNDERSCORED WITH MAHOGANY IN ELEGANTLY TRADITIONAL ROOM

You can copy
a color scheme

Everywhere you look—in your friends' homes, in the model rooms of your favorite store, in smart new offices, or a gaily re-decorated drugstore, in a fine restaurant, in the pages of magazines, pamphlets, and books—in all these places you find ideas for your own home. Sometimes it's a way of arranging a few pieces of furniture, or of hanging a picture, or an interesting window treatment that catches your eye.

Often, the idea that strikes your particular fancy is a fresh and exciting color scheme. Even though it is in a room very different from your own, you *can* copy it, and adapt it to your own family tastes.

Analyze colors

First, analyze all the colors in the room. What is the one note that sets the theme? Is it the drapery fabric, the floor covering—a picture, a color, or a wallpaper pattern?

List the colors you find—as an example, red and pink on a white background, with a rose-red carpet, pink walls, stark white accessories, underscored with ebony wood tones. Which of these colors is dark, which is light—which is dull, which is bright?

Analyze color proportions

Then, pay special attention to the proportions of each color used. Which cover the greatest area, which serve a moderate area, which are accents? Now you can transpose this scheme to your own home, in your own style, to suit your own tastes.

The brilliance of smaller amounts of dominant pattern accents large neutral areas

Although the big, bold fabric pattern is less than 10 percent of this room's color, it is the dominating force, accentuated by the pale background shell. From its mixture of black, green, gray, white, and earth-brown, all other colors are derived. Dark and medium wood tones pick up the brown, as do the pottery lamp bases and planters.

Soft gray appears in textured walls, carpeting, solid-toned draperies which frame the view. Big pictures contain these colors, too. Growing plants pick up the green tones. A splash of brilliant golden flowers brightens the subtle scheme.

Bathroom colors are inspired by same Provincial scheme

If your bathroom fixtures are white, you'll want your area of brilliant pattern to feature white, too, so one area relates to the other.

Here, the accent pattern is concentrated into one spot because the room is very small. The dominant light red is carried to the floor in the bath rug, to the opposite wall with bright red, white towels. Walls are straw-colored, the hard-surfaced flooring a bit darker.

This color adaptation sparks a drab old bedroom

Bleach the old bedroom furniture down to a straw tone, paper or paint the walls and ceiling. Add texture with a white-on-white bedspread, thick scatter rugs, filmy curtains.

Maybe you'd prefer the accent fabric in emerald green or bright blue instead of in the original red. Here, the accent covers a headboard, slipper chair, and cornice. A softer blue in the lamp shades helps distribute color throughout the room.

A budget variation translates scheme into a small room

The same dramatic effects as in the room at the right are easy to achieve in a contemporary setting. Use white sheeting or dress material for draperies, coarse-textured cloth in sand tones for sofa, honey-colored furniture, straw matting on the floor.

Then splurge on a few yards of brilliantly bold fabric to accent the chairs. Include an eye-catching picture that picks up fabric colors, and use strong black accents.

Soft, light colors stress textures, brilliant accents

Large areas of subtly combined white and straw tones are a dramatic foil for a vivid splash of color. The accent fabric could be changed to another vibrant color, and the pattern flowered rather than plaid—but it must remain emphatic. Accessories are important.

Same colors, proportions, translate into dining area

Here's a way to vary the basic idea. The colors are used in almost the same proportions, in the same areas. The pattern is still in the floor, but a bright, clear yellow is combined with a brown flooring stripe.

The coral is used for chair seats, repeated in the lamp shade. Again, yellow meets yellow in table and wall. White and yellow meet at the corner, are interrupted only by the accent of blue-lined shelves.

Different textures vary this color interpretation

Again, yellow and white adjoin each other, this time with crisp, sheer draperies and textured brick instead of the smoother, flat surfaces of the original. Contact of floor and draperies adds yellow against yellow.

Pattern is still in the rug, this time in wood-brown, sparked with coral. A coral spread covers the couch. The same warm tone accents the hanging Japanese lantern. Yellow pillow is additional accent.

Pattern goes up, color areas remain the same

This time, the pattern is on the bedspread instead of the floor, but the color areas stay proportionately the same. Yellow against yellow, and white against white, reappear in the meeting of ceiling and wall, ceiling and wood paneling.

Bright coral hugs the floor, is repeated in the flower centers of the bedspread. A crisp color scheme like this goes a long way in sprucing up a down-at-the-heels room.

The basic formula here: stress yellow, solid colors, bold areas of clean color

The largest area of color is pure yellow, with a little less white, accents of blue, black, and coral. Only pattern is the coral and yellow rug. Notice how the yellow sofa is used against the yellow wall, how white and yellow meet in the corner, how coral jumps up to accent the sofa pillows, lamp shade, and hassock.

This adaptation features bold use of plaid

The informal mood of the original room has been kept in this adaptation of the original color scheme for a family room-porch.

This patterned floor could be a fiber rug, linoleum, or tile. Bamboo furniture, blinds, and the mellow woodwork echo the golden maple tones. Upholstery fabric picks up color from plaid, makes massive pieces look smaller. Bright accents give vibrant contrast to soft colors.

The plaid pattern stays on wall in this version

Once you've analyzed the basic color idea, you can adapt it to almost any room, any styling, any taste.

Here, one bold pattern—dominating plaid wallpaper—is the catalyst. Warm honey tones appear in the tables and chairs, in the paneling of the kitchen area.

Hard-surfaced floor repeats the coloring of the original room. The counter tops, dishes, and table linens supply smaller areas of contrasting accent color.

A fabric pattern supplies the dominant force here

Again, plaid dominates room, this time in a fabric used for cornice, draperies, and slip covers. Green walls relate to the dark tones of the plaid—in a dark room, this could be changed to a lighter color.

Honey shades appear in the bamboo blind and the corner table, with contrasting texture in the smooth-surfaced lamp shade. The floor covering is neutral—and accents on table and wall add extra color.

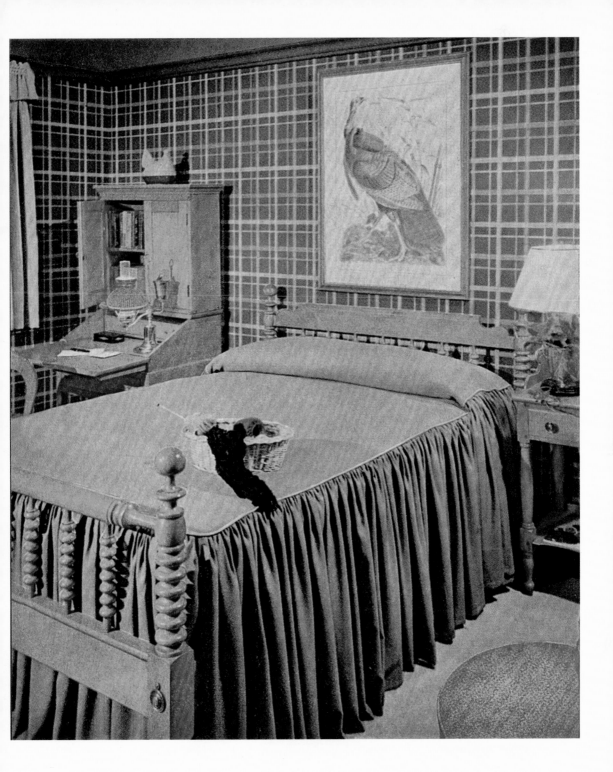

Scheme uses large areas of plaid, repeats hues

This formula of plaid teamed with plain is an easy one to copy—the only trick is figuring where and why the plains are used. Green dominates, next is the golden tone of the maple, and the neutral of the rug. Vivid red is used sparingly, while the blue-green of the bedspread relates to the background of plaid wallpaper.

Blue and lavender reverse positions in this adaptation

The formula at right is (1) massed white (2) splashes of lavender (3) lesser amounts of aqua and blue.

In this fresh Colonial bedroom, walls, ruffle, table top, cushion of white keep it the dominant color. Blue and aqua move up to second place in spread, carpet, and draperies.

Lavender takes third place, appears as an accent in drapery fabric and bench cushion. Silvery metal of original scheme turns to more authentic brass. Black is a strong accent.

Lavender moves from walls to floor in this dining room

The original proportions of color are maintained in this Contemporary version of the scheme. White is again dominant, on walls and ceiling, in curtains, in background of drapery fabric. Lavender moves to floor in a dramatic expanse of carpeting, is repeated in chair upholstery. Shades of blue sharply accent other chair seats and buffet candles.

Brass gleams as the shining metal texture, while all the colors are strengthened by color of the wood.

Blue-green flatters walls— white adds freshness

Typical of their French Provincial origin, sofa and chair frames, tables, lamps, are white, complement expanse of white carpeting . . . made practical by today's easy-care fibers.

Blue-green takes second place— beautifies the painted walls. Lavender covers the sofa, is repeated in the drapery swag.

The green of plants in the original scheme is picked up for a second side chair, and a touch of red is brought in for the desk chair cushion.

Lavender, aqua, and blue sparkle against white

The dominant color in this distinctive scheme is white, massed on the floor, in the draperies and area rug. Next in quantity is lavender, on walls and chair. Blues are present in lesser amounts, on stools, rug. Silver and black accents complete the color plan.

Consider the compass
when planning color schemes

NORTH: *Cool light*
requires warmth in color

Colors retain their purity best of all under a north light—which is why artists always try to work in such surroundings. But this light is cool, so that you should use lots of warm tones to bring a feeling of friendliness to the room.

The large color areas—your walls, floor, and the major upholstered pieces, can be gayer and brighter than in rooms facing any other direction. Use cool colors for smaller pieces and for accessories, accents, to give necessary balance.

WEST: *Afternoon*
sun calls for cool colors

Even though it's in shade for part of the day, the rich reds, oranges, and yellows of the evening sky give warmth to a west room.

It's well to think of color in medium values—between the bright and the dull, the warm and the cool. For example, if your favorite color is green, be sure that there are big areas of cool green, then spark them with tones in upholstery that are on the yellow side. Keep bright accessories to a minimum, select most in neutral dark shades.

Before making a decision on the ingredients of your color scheme, consider one more factor—the direction your rooms face. Basically, rooms facing north and east should be keyed with warm colors, rooms facing south and west "live" best in cooler tones. You can fit your favorite colors into any room, if color in the large areas follows this suggestion. Select these tones for daylight use—plan artificial lighting to enhance them at night.

EAST: *Divide colors between warm and cool*

As in the case of a west room, an eastern exposure is in shade part of the day. But the rising sun's rays are essentially cooler than those of the later day, and you will probably prefer to apportion your colors about two-thirds on the warm side, one-third cool.

If your choice is a cool green or blue, use it as pattern against a neutral background, and as accents, with largest areas in tones from sunny side of color palette. Spark with black and white.

SOUTH: *Keep colors grayed for this exposure*

The hottest, brightest light for most of the day comes from the sun moving into a south room. Here you will be flooded with the happy gaiety of summer, get most of your winter richness of yellow light.

You will probably want some brightness in your color scheme, too, but keep it to a minimum, with the largest areas in dull, absorbing, cool tones. Vary these with neutrals, and keep color combinations simple. A one-color scheme is effective in warm rooms.

How to use
the same scheme
all through
the house

By using one-color scheme in varying shades and amounts throughout your home, you can create an illusion of spaciousness. This also allows you to interchange furniture from one room to another, pull a bedroom chair up to the dining-room table or retire the living room rug to the bedroom.

Here's how you can build the one-color-scheme look from room to room. First, choose the color combination that you'll use in every room. Then decide on the background, secondary, and accent tones for each room.

Living room colors set pace

The blue of walls and floor coverings stems from the blue of the fabric. Violet is picked up for the sofa, with purple, deeper blue, and bittersweet used for the other furnishings and for accents.

Kitchen colors are vibrant

Vivid new color scheme for the kitchen takes its colors from the living room fabric, too. Pink counter tops and matching walls sharpen the violet cabinets. The soft blue of the floor tile is echoed in canisters and pottery trim, carried up to the ceiling for the final color touch.

Dining colors are unified

The fabric is used again in the dining room, giving the interior a unified look from outside. This time brick-patterned wallpaper gives a textured look to the white background.

The rose-red of the fabric is used for carpeting, and repeated in lusters on the buffet. Chair seats are deep blue—both a practical and handsome choice. White pots hold greens, violets to carry out the color scheme.

Bedroom colors are restful

Drapery fabric used again, this time for a bright spread. The floor is the same blue tile used in the kitchen, sparked with violet throw rugs. Pillows; drapery lining, and lamp shade are pink, while a sharper red accents the comfortable chair.

You can plan a one-color scheme without monotony

There are two applications of one-color schemes—one is literally just that, and called monochromatic. It is confined to shades and tones of the same basic color, with bright accents used sparingly. This color plan is usually found in just one room. The other one-color scheme is the use of one basic color throughout the house in varying shades and tones, but in different amounts in each room, so that there is no sameness or tedium.

Cool blue sets the theme for this house   Blue in the floor, the rug, and the walls accounts for about 75 per cent of the color in this living room. Strong pink and white divide the balance of large areas about equally. Red is the accent color.

Blue, pink, white
—in equal amounts

Pink shares honors with basic blue and white. Blue walls and doors in the dining room, kitchen cabinets, account for about one-third of the color. Pink kitchen wall and sweep of floor are another third. Balance is in white rug, kitchen ceiling. Deeper pink is again the accent—in counter tops, kitchen accessories, chair seats.

The first kind of one-color scheme—the monochromatic—is particularly useful where you want a shell background for one dramatic piece. This could be a brilliant fabric in drapery or upholstery, an elegantly ornamented breakfront or chest.

It is also of great service in making small rooms seem larger, because there is never a definite break in any color line, from floor to walls to ceiling. The plan suits the contemporary open architecture, too, lets the eye range from one living area to another without interruption.

The other one-color plan is a little more complicated, but not difficult to execute, as shown on pages 102-103. Start with the color you want to live with—blue or green, pink or red,

yellow, brown or gray. Since it is the basis of your color planning, you will probably want to use it in large quantities in your living room. Plan its quality there—should it be bright or dull, dark or light? Should it be on the warm side of the color wheel, or with a touch of coolness? When you have made your choice, it's always wise to start your buying with a floor covering, since you can match or blend wall colors with it easily.

Plan family rooms first

Since the rooms where all the family—and your friends—gather are really the most important, start your color planning with the living room, then the dining room and kitchen.

Using a one-color scheme

Y ou've established the proportions of your favorite colors in the rooms where family and friends meet. Now carry them on into the other rooms in the house. In the master bedroom they can have a formal feeling, dignified, restful. In the children's rooms, select these same colors in fabrics and furnishings that are simple and easy

to keep, won't show dirt or wrinkles. In the nursery, use bright accent tones for the major areas, because little children thrive under strong color—prefer it to pastels.

In the bathroom, be sure to include the color of your fixtures—white or pastels—in shower curtain, rug or wallpaper pattern.

Red replaces pink as main color in master bedroom

Just as in the living room on page 104, about 75 per cent of the color here is blue, with white and red sharing the rest of the major areas. Pink replaces red as the accent in this room.

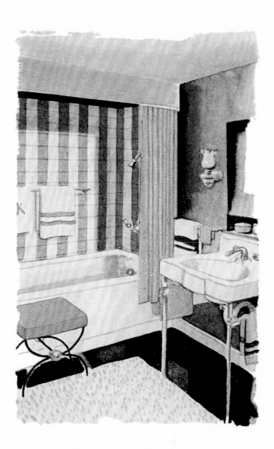

Paler shades, much white, distinguish bathroom

A bathroom is a place for make-up and shaving, needs pale colors so that light will reflect properly. The largest areas here are in white. Walls are a pale blue—the dominant color of the house—with gay pink ceiling, stool cover and towels. The same dark blue used in the living room is found in hard-surfaced floor, to provide the "something dark" every color scheme should have. Bright red accents in other rooms could be used for bottles, towels, other accessories.

Television-guest room is bright but easy to keep

Here is a room sturdy enough for the whole family to relax in—handsome enough to be an inviting guest room. Blue is again the major color, accounting for about 75 per cent of the color area. This time the darker shade is in the practical slip cover and tiered draperies, with a lighter tone used on the walls.

White is the second major color, in curtains, and the scrubbable paint of the built-in back of the bed. Bright red accents the scheme, with pink at a minimum.

Floor could be random boards or a plank-patterned linoleum.

Now let's build some
color schemes

This family is in the young junior executive bracket, and, where home furnishings are concerned, interested in Contemporary design, antiques, and Oriental pieces.

Their home is planned for easy care and informal living. They like the brightness of contemporary colors, the easy-to-keep qualities of modern fabrics and finishes.

Decide background colors

Our family especially liked a subtly colored rug in a modern design, combined with a resilient flooring that blends tones of browns and beiges, doesn't show marks or spills.

While their home was being built, they included walls of rich texture, in soft wood and white painted brick. To enhance the qualities of these two design elements, they repeated the natural wood tones of the rug and flooring in the paneling, picked up white in the rug for the brick.

Select furniture colors

The colors of furniture frames and tables again emphasize wood tones. Smoothly textured sofa upholstery echos the white in the rug.

Chairs are covered in a gleaming yellow—again picked up from the rug—soft enough to blend with the beiges and whites of the room.

1 *Rich textures soften a palette of beiges*

A variety of textures highlights this all-of-a-color scheme, with tones ranging from creamy white to deep chocolate. The area rug carries related values of yellow and orange, a basis for selection of accent and accessory colors in the later planning stages of the color scheme.

2 *Furniture tones follow the basic color theme*

Drawn from the colors of the rug, but adding a brilliant, smooth effect to the original rougher textures, tables and chairs, sofa and fireplace enhance the pattern of the rug. Framed by solid color, the rug pattern stands out, takes on new importance in the scheme.

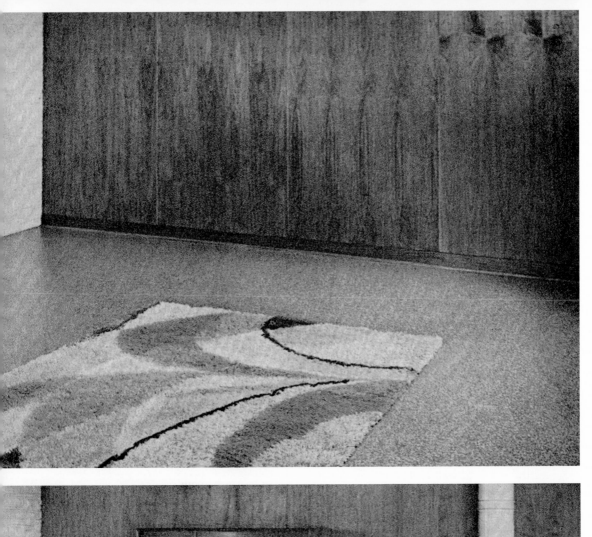

Choosing accessories, accents

The first two of the three steps to color-scheming are selection of background colors, and then the selection of colors for the major furniture pieces. In this room, the variety of off-white to brown tones chosen for the walls and the flooring, emphasizes, also blends with, the dominant rug pattern, and the lighter, brighter upholstery colors.

Select accent colors

The third, and final, step is the selection of the bright accent colors that give sparkle and life to a room.

Because the bright colors of the rug are the yellows and oranges, they're intensified for flowers, pillows, tea service, and for the fruits.

Other accessories pick up the more subtle tones of the background and the white of wall and fireplace. An idea to copy—the picture hung on the open shelf in the cabinet, serving as a concealing sliding door.

Something dark and light

As most well-decorated rooms should be, this one is balanced between dark and light, dull and bright.

3 Distribute accents throughout the room

The distribution of accent colors around the room is just as important as using the right color. For greatest effectiveness and to give it importance, place a mass of accent color in one spot.

Here, the accent's in the massive arrangement of the flowers near the fireplace—also in the smaller quantities elsewhere in the room . . . here, in a pillow, in book bindings, in cups.

finishes your color-scheme planning

Let's build a

traditional scheme

This home belongs to a well-established, young/middle-aged couple. They have a teen-age daughter, a slightly younger son, and a well-behaved dachshund who rules the household. They prefer Traditional design, are wedded to comfort.

But, with the children and their friends gathering night and day, and with a full social schedule of their own, they insist on the most modern work-free materials. They want their home to retain its traditional elegance, but be easy to maintain.

Light colors are practical

New scrubbable paints that resist finger marks, easily cleaned carpeting, fabric finishes that scorn dust, repel stains . . . these permit the use of delicate color, combine good looks with the easiest care.

Unequal color is interesting

The precept that color in unequal amounts is more pleasing, is well demonstrated here. Pale, but vibrant, blue on the walls is the dominant color, balanced in smaller amounts with the sage-green of the carpet, and white in the fabric pattern and the fireplace. The blues and greens in the upholstery fabric tie all of the background colors together.

1 *Decorating theme is based on subtle pattern*

A traditional flowered fabric pattern, used on the sofa, contains the basic colors for the room. From it are drawn the dominant blue for the walls, the brownish-green for the carpeting. Its white background lightens the room, is used again as an accent and accessory color.

2 *Deep wood tones lend dignity to the room*

Chosen both for color and for style, the tables here reflect a brownish tone in the fabric, blend with the pattern in setting the elegant traditional theme. The lounge chair is covered in another of the brownish-green tones picked up from the fabric, adds texture to room.

Bright accents spark this

Our dignified-but-hospitable family chose a traditional background for themselves, in light, basically cool colors, in walls, carpet, and fabric.

Warm accents give balance

The two major colors, blue and brownish green, are both from the cool color side of the color wheel.

For a pleasing balance, deep crimson was chosen for flowers, tawny tones for fruit, the gleaming gold tones of brass for the fireplace firedogs, fender and tools. Proper lighting adds to the cheerfulness of the fire.

A magnificent classic print, in a deepened tone of the carpet, is shot with strong blue, pulls the color scheme together on the wall which backs the print-covered sofa.

Some accessories are neutral

Black, white, and silver tones are neutral in effect, so they can be used with any combination of other colors. Here, they provide necessary form without introducing another tone. They also give variety of texture, from the roughness of the sculpture on the chimney breast, to the polished surfaces of statue and obelisk.

3 Stick to one bright color for the accents

Since there are already two definite colors in this room — blue and green, plus the brown tones of the woods, one bright accent is all that's needed. Here it's red — in flowers and fruit.

At other seasons, other times, it might be impressive pieces of cranberry glass, or crimson pieces of china. The color can also change . . . yellow or orange would be equally effective.

fresh traditional color scheme

Think before you buy

← wrong

*Don't buy misfits
just because they
strike your fancy*

See what happens when you forget your basic decorating theme! As right as this carpeting might be in another room with a different furniture style, it's definitely out of place in this Colonial bedroom. In both color and pattern, the bedspread and carpeting compete.

right →

*Once you've decided
on a color plan—
stick with it*

A harmonious color scheme is the result of pre-planning—and perseverance. Don't buy on impulse! Here, walls, carpeting, window treatment, and furniture blend in color and style. Orange, yellow, toast tones, used throughout the room, stem from the cheerful plaid bedspread.

Create convenience with
furniture
arrangement

The basic "rule"
of furniture arrangement
is comfort. Here are 42 pages of ideas on how
to fit furniture into any home—large or
small, luxurious, or decorated on a budget

Pages 117 through 158

Every room problem has a solution

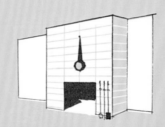

Establish a center of interest

Dramatize one spot in your room, and arrange furniture to draw attention to it. This center of decorating interest can be the fireplace, or a lovely garden view, or perhaps an exciting picture arrangement

Discover the paths traffic takes

Make a floor plan of your room, then sketch in the traffic lanes—the obvious paths by which people get in and out of the room. Arrange furniture so no traffic lane can disturb a conversational grouping by passing through it

Consider scale and balance

Plan furnishings so that chairs, tables, accessories, are the right size for each other. Balance room so heavy pieces are not all in one spot, light ones in another

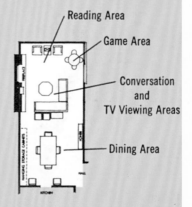

Reading Area

Game Area

Conversation and TV Viewing Areas

Dining Area

Plan rooms for more than one use

Make the most of a big room, or a long, narrow one. Arrange furniture so games, dining, conversation, television viewing, reading, or studying have separate, undisturbed areas. See that each area is not disturbed by traffic

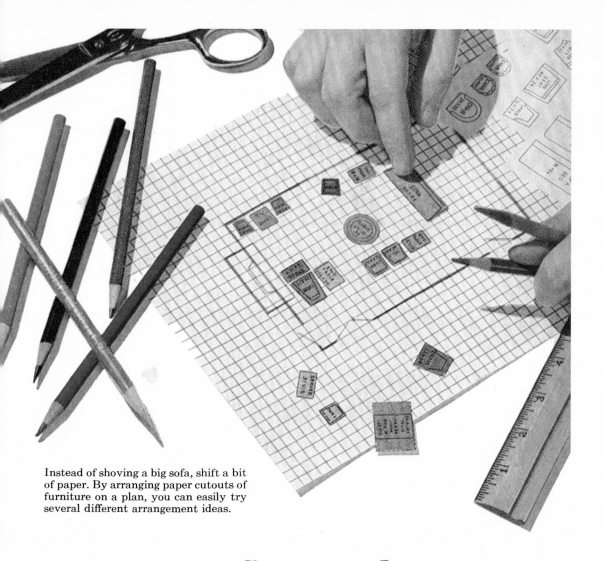

Instead of shoving a big sofa, shift a bit of paper. By arranging paper cutouts of furniture on a plan, you can easily try several different arrangement ideas.

Start with a floor plan

Whether you are just rearranging the furniture you already have, or are buying new pieces, start with your present floor plan.

Sketch the outlines of your room on graph paper, indicating windows and doors and the direction in which the doors open. It's a good idea to show electrical outlets, too. Then figure out the traffic lanes.

Next, make paper patterns of the furniture pieces you own—and those you plan to buy. Or, you can use the graph paper and furniture pieces that are on pages 393 through 397.

This planning ahead will show you just the sizes you will need in the new pieces you expect to buy and save you time and effort in rearranging your present furniture.

Plan for rooms with fireplaces

$\rightarrow$

Consider the need for open floor space in a small, square room

A square room is almost always a small room, too, which makes it even more difficult to decorate. Be careful to conserve your limited floor space—use chairside tables instead of coffee tables which would swallow up the scarce footages in the center of the room. If the traffic pattern moves across one end, arrange the furniture along the walls adjoining the fireplace wall. The arrows point up how the traffic lanes from the three entrances have been kept free from congestion.

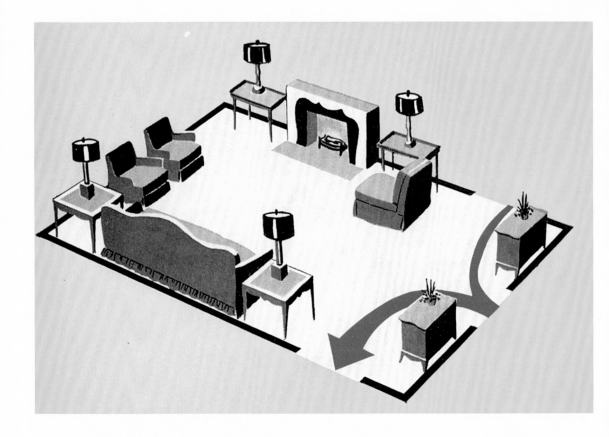

$\rightarrow$

A big, rectangular room calls for separation of living areas

Conversational groupings need to be placed so that people can talk comfortably, not have to shout. In a big, rectangular room with a traffic lane through the middle, place such a grouping at one end, around the fireplace and out of the way of through-room traffic. The other end of the room may be used as a study or a letter-writing area, for a music or a hobby corner. A divider could be used here to good effect, standing across the room, separating the room into distinct areas.

←

Plan furniture groupings to cut length of long narrow room

To avoid the bowling-alley look of a long, narrow room, arrange the furniture to cut the length. Place a chair, a desk, or a sofa at right angles to the wall, preferably backing the traffic lane and creating a "hall." Then a more intimate conversation grouping can be arranged around the fireplace in the remaining portion of the room. Here, a storage wall with built-in television would fit in one of the unused corners. The big lounge chair by the fireplace might be a swivel.

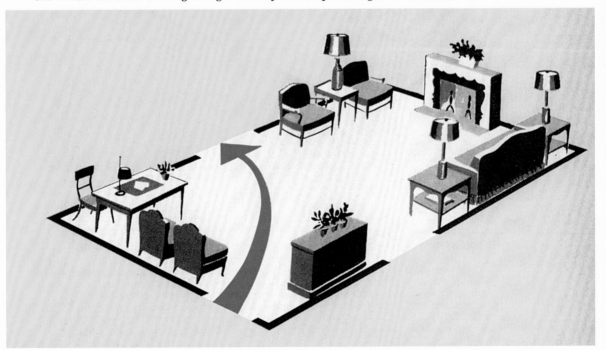

Plan for rooms without fireplaces

→

In this rectangular room, a chair-chest grouping is focal point

A big, rectangular room will offer plenty of space for a center of interest. You can make a focal point of bookcases, a window treatment, or just an interesting grouping of pictures above the sofa. In this room, two wing chairs and a pair of chests at the end of the room act as the focal point. Hang a dramatic picture arrangement or some other grouping above the chests. Following the traffic arrow, you move smoothly past the desk and chairs without disturbing conversation.

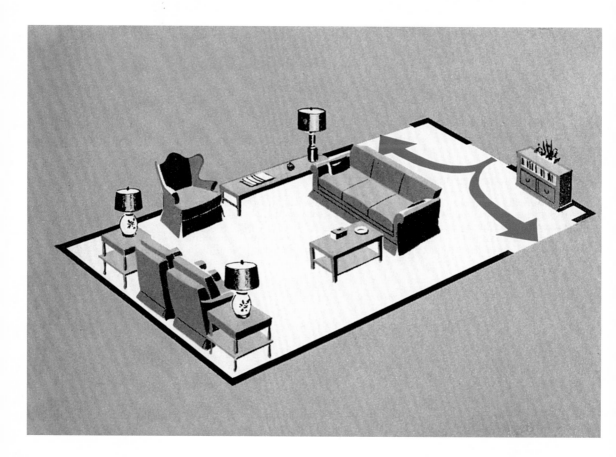

→

A massive focal point helps to alter the shape of a square room

A square room needs a heavy focal point to minimize its boxy look, to make the room appear longer. You can get a center of interest by pushing some long, low bookcases underneath a pair of well-dressed windows. Place a conversation grouping on either side of the window arrangement. If there are no windows on the opposite wall, balance the focal point with a large picture or a mirror. Then you can use the other wall areas for a writing desk or another major grouping of chairs.

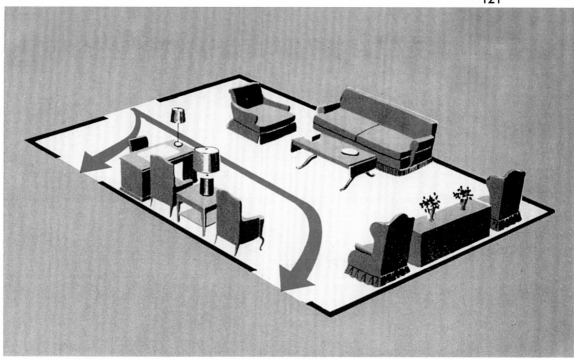

Long, narrow room seems wider with a compact arrangement

To make your long, narrow rooms seem wider, let the bulkiest furniture jut into the room at right angles to the longest walls. This seems to create the feeling of another wall there. If the sofa stands with its back to the traffic lane, the length of the room will be cut even more. Create your point of decorating emphasis on the end wall opposite the sofa. Here, pairs of chairs and end tables catch the eye. Complement this group with a series of pictures, or a dramatic sweep of draperies.

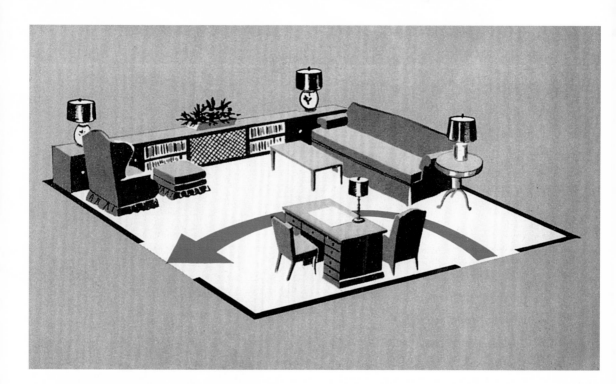

Well-planned furniture layout

The furniture arrangement in this house takes into account the normal traffic pattern. The patterns, shown on page 124, dictate just where each piece goes. There is an unobstructed path in and out of each room; closets are easily accessible; conversational groupings are out of the way; and window walls are left uncluttered.

Start with your
traffic pattern . . .
then place furniture,
plan for color

makes maximum use of space

Decorating is "good" only if it is practical as well as beautiful. Furniture looks its best when it is placed in accordance with obvious traffic patterns—creates a subtle feeling of comfort and hospitality.

Good traffic patterns indicate
how furniture should be arranged

1. Entry divides flow of traffic to major areas.

2. Natural path to bedroom patio avoids furniture.

3. Hallway gives children access to bedrooms, kitchen, family room, terrace, without disturbing adult part of the house.

4. Terrace is accessible from family or living areas.

5. Path crosses conversation groups, but area is for adults, more formal entertaining. Groups will probably be moving as a unit to dining room or terrace.

6. There's access from the kitchen to all areas, easy serving to dining room, living room.

7. Area serves only living room, so cross traffic is not important to seating comfort.

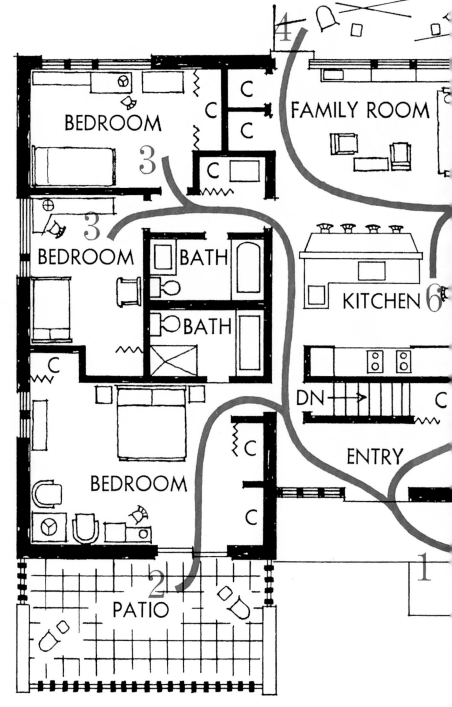

BEDROOM

FAMILY ROOM

C C C C

BEDROOM BATH

BATH

KITCHEN

DN

BEDROOM

ENTRY

PATIO

This is the basic floor plan of the home on page 122, with the normal flow of traffic indicated. You can see at a glance how these fixed patterns help you to decide where to place your furniture, and in some cases show you just what that furniture should be.

If you are buying or building, a quick sketch of a traffic pattern will be a tremendous help in determining whether the house is planned for convenience and comfort.

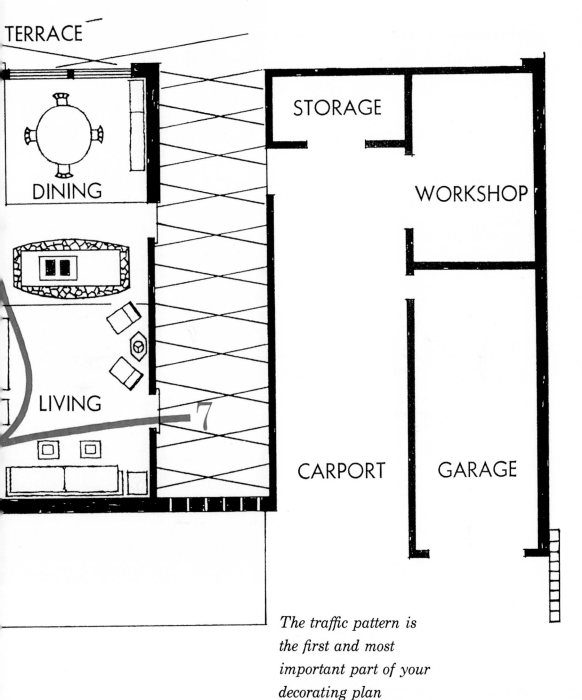

TERRACE

DINING

LIVING

STORAGE

WORKSHOP

CARPORT   GARAGE

The traffic pattern is the first and most important part of your decorating plan

Establish a decorative center of interest

Now you have established your traffic patterns, and that in turn has decided where your furnishings are going to go, what sizes they will be—and, to some extent, the placement of color in your room. Next comes the decision as to where and what your "center of interest" is to be.

The center of interest is that part of your room which you wish to play up—make dramatic—make the focal point of your decorating. It can be an architecturally natural spot, such as a fireplace, or a picture window with a view. Or, it can be an arranged spot, such as a wall of built-ins, with your sofa nestled in the center. It can be a magnificent picture on a long wall, which catches the eye as soon as someone walks into the room, and draws them to it.

The center can vary

Sometimes you may want to plan your center of interest so that it can change with the seasons. In summer you may be able to look out onto your garden. Then, of course, that view will be your focal point. In the winter, the same furnishings may be turned to face a fireplace.

There can always be at least one center of interest in every room, either architectural or arranged. Find your natural spot for decorating emphasis, or plan one, before you decide on your color theme or arrangement.

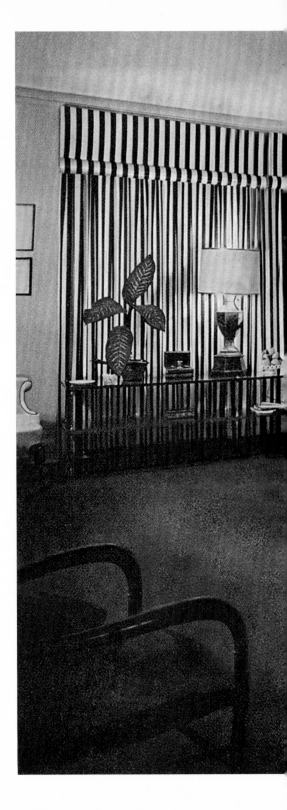

The fireplace serves as the center of interest in this living room

The fireplace provides a natural center of interest. Twin sofas are arranged so that this grouping is the major one. They seat four comfortably, with pull-up chairs to serve a larger group. Coffee table can be used for fireside dining — will also serve the pull-up chairs when company comes. Colors are bold, to dramatize this impor-

tant spot. Bold is massed in the sofa upholstery, emphasized again in floral arrangements, distributed across the room in lamp base, fruit, and flowers. Plants and pictures pick up green of the carpet.

Notice how traffic will bypass this grouping. It comes through the door, past the windows, never in front of anyone seated.

People require space, too, so leave some room for them when planning arrangements

Conversation groups

Sitting down for a nice chat is a lot more fun if you don't have to shout across the wide, open spaces. For easy sociability—and for normal hearing—there should be approximately eight feet between conversation groups. Any more than that, and you'll have to strain your voice to be heard, sit forward in your chair to catch the conversation.

Getting up from the table

Give the man a chance to be gallant! Getting up from the table uses up 30 inches. And he'll need sufficient room to walk behind your chair, too. In all, that requires a minimum of 54 inches from the wall. Give yourself room to serve and to clear the table. Children will need even more space than adults need.

Pulling out a drawer

You'll need about 36 inches to stand in front of even a partly opened drawer. This is the minimum amount of space, and you'll probably want enough room to open the drawer completely. You'll avoid frustrating moments if you keep this in mind when arranging furniture with drawers that pull out.

Passing between furniture

For one normal-size adult, you will need to leave a 30-inch traffic lane. Comfortable passing between two pieces of furniture requires that much.

If it's the traffic lane from the kitchen, you'll need enough extra space to accommodate trays, plates, and elbows, too. When planning traffic lanes around doorways, always be sure to allow space for several people to pass at once.

Sitting at a coffee table

If the family is of usual size, be sure to allow 15 inches between chair or sofa and your coffee table. Otherwise, watch out for bruises, barked shins.

Remember . . . the first rule of furniture arrangement is "comfort." That means comfortable sitting and convenience for all the family and guests.

Consider scale and balance when decorating your home

Scale and balance are factors so common in decorating that we are not aware of them until they are absent. It is easy to put them to work for you, if you will just stop a minute and study what they mean.

1. *Scale means the ratio of the size of the individual parts (arms, back, seat, legs) to each other.*

Check the measurements of each part of the sofa or chair before you buy it. This doesn't mean to write down feet-and-inches dimensions. But check them by sitting down on the sofa or chair. Make sure that the height of the seat and arms is comfortable, the seat is not too deep or too close to the floor, the arms are not too high or too far apart. Be sure that the scale of the chair or sofa is right in relationship to you and your family.

2. *Scale means the over-all dimensions of each piece as compared to the size of other furniture in the same room.*

For instance, big end tables require big lamps; small lamps belong on tiny tables. An oversize sofa requires other furniture of some mass in the room.

3. *Scale means the relationship of each piece to the size of the room where it is placed.*

Small pieces belong in a small room because they give the room spaciousness and grace. Large rooms, on the other hand, demand large massive pieces, strong colors, and large designs. They give strength and dignity.

The general term, "balance," refers to the restful-looking effect you get when shapes and colors are placed around a center point. You get balance in two ways:

A *Formal, or symmetrical, balance results when all the objects on one side of a central line are repeated on the other side, the same distance from the center.*

Imagine a child's teeter-totter, balanced exactly in the middle, with a child of equal weight on either end. This type is easiest to achieve; it's restful—and conservative.

B *Informal, or asymmetrical, balance results when unlike elements are used on each side of a center point and at different distances from the center.*

Again, imagine a child's teeter-totter, but this time with one end very long the other very short. On the long end will be balanced the lighter child, on the short end will be the heavier child. This kind of balance is varied.

Balance applies to color, too.

If you were to use a plain beige carpet, plain beige walls, and plain beige upholstery in a room, the effect would be very dull. But if you add two or more brighter colors, such as red or green, you would produce a more pleasing balance.

Formal balance—everything in pairs

Every item in this room is in perfect formal balance. The sofa and the tall picture above it serve as the fulcrum. On either side, matching end tables hold matching lamps. Lounge chairs, exactly alike, face each other across the coffee table. Pictures, framed alike, line up on either side of the center, forming a solid oblong that balances the sofa.

Informal balance within a formal frame

At first glance, this room also is in perfect formal balance. Again, pairs of end tables, lamps, and chairs appear. The picture grouping over the sofa is, in its entirety, balanced formally to the sofa. But variety is gained, and informal balance introduced, by the pictures. The biggest frame is in the upper corner, with smaller ones grouped around it.

Here is informal balance in furnishings

This is a good example of informal balance, and the variety it can give a room. The sofa is still the fulcrum of this group. On one side is an end table, with a lamp. On the other is a floor lamp, tall enough and massive enough to balance the end table. One chair has square arms and is covered in a plaid. The other is covered in a plain textured fabric.

Scale lamps to tables

Tables should be selected to insure comfort. An easy chair needs a table for there are always books, magazines, and ash trays to cope with.

For convenience, a table should be approximately the height of the arm of the chair by which it is used. When seated, it is uncomfortable to have to reach up or down when you want an object on the table.

Consider the function of the table before deciding how large a top surface it should have. The decorative aspects of a table are important but keep in mind where and how you will use it, and then choose accordingly.

The same requirements for comfort guide you in the selection of lamps for your rooms. The choices of color and style are personal ones. But apply the same yardsticks of placement and size that you did in selecting your tables.

Most seating arrangements need adequate illumination. The lamp you select should be of sufficient size and height to cast enough light on the reading and working areas.

Balance and scale are important when combining lamps and tables.

This table is too low and too small for comfortable use

Every chair deserves the *right* size table. This one is too low. The lamp and ash trays are likely to be pushed off.

The table is also too delicately scaled for such a massive chair. The top surface is too small to hold all of the items usually needed next to a lounge chair—lamp, ash trays, books.

This lamp is too low to throw enough light for reading

Every table deserves the *right* size lamp. Now the table is exactly suitable for the chair, but the lamp, while handsome in design, is not a good choice for the table and chair.

The light falls only over the arm of the chair. A lamp should be tall enough, and the shade big enough to throw plenty of light on handwork, reading material, surrounding area.

A table can serve more than one chair

Twin chairs plus a long, low coffee table make an attractive grouping for conversation or reading.

A large box base added to the lamp raises it to a more correct height. This arrangement could also serve as a room divider.

This table is just the right size and height for its chair

The table that's selected for any chair should be of the right scale and proportion to the size of the chair itself. It should be approximately the same height as the arm of the chair, and its surface should be large enough to hold all the necessary items. For a reading chair, a table with a shelf for books is a particularly good choice.

This lamp will send a wide gleam of light over work or reading

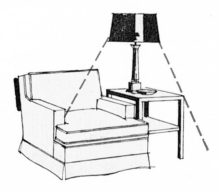

When you're out shopping for new tables and lamps, take your chair measurements with you. First, select the table, and then the lamp. Every table should have a lamp that is good for reading, one that lights up the whole chair area. Now we have the right chair, the right table, and the right lamp, all together in one place. The result is years of comfortable service.

Where do you put your television set?

The first consideration, as in all furniture arrangement, is comfort. The set should be placed where the whole family can see it easily, where there is no glare on the screen. There should be seating units for everyone, and they should be comfortable.

Placement is important. Plan the seating arrangement so that everyone has an unobstructed view of the set, without twisting and turning.

Leave at least one light burning where it will not be reflected onto the face of the set. Proper lighting prevents unnecessary eyestrain.

Place a comfortable chair near the set, so that one viewer can work the controls without getting up.

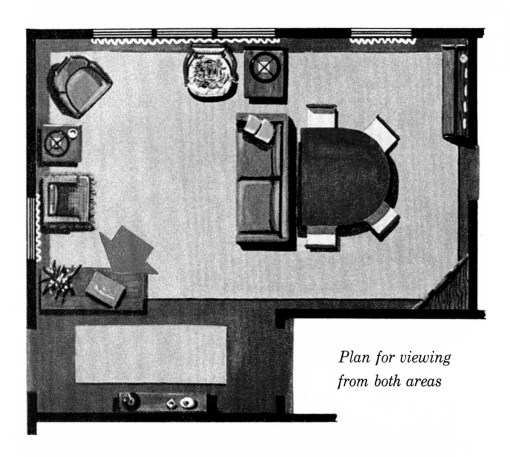

*Plan for viewing
from both areas*

Here's good planning for a family room, where you will be eating informally as well as just lounging. Placed on a cabinet, the set becomes an integral, unobtrusive part of the center-of-interest arrangement. It serves the entire living area, is easily seen even from the chair on the left wall. The set also serves the dining area, can be enjoyed while the table is in use for hobbies or guests.

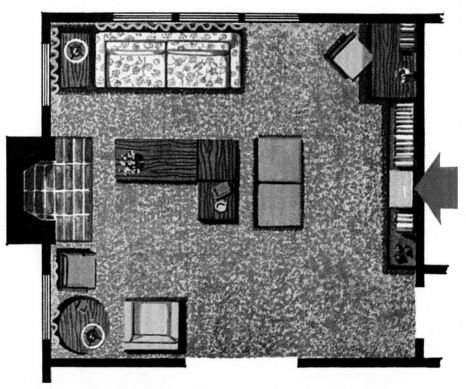

In a more formal living room, the set again becomes part of a center-of-interest arrangement. Upholstered pull-up benches at the right of the coffee table are low enough to see over, move for extra seating if guests wish to watch a special show. Convenient plan serves both the fireplace wall and the cabinet-television set arrangement.

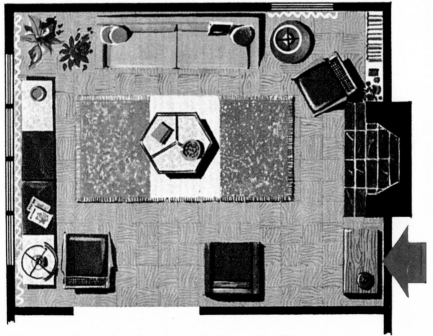

There is really only one place for a television set in this room — near the fireplace. Because it must stand alone here, a cabinet set was chosen, important in its own right as a piece of furniture, big enough to become part of the center-of-interest wall. Programs can be viewed from every seat in the room, without moving furniture.

Every home should be furnished to suit the tastes and

the living pattern of the people occupying it.

This snug home belongs to the Green family.

Relaxed home for quiet tastes

The Green family live in a cozy, comfortable Colonial house which reflects their conservative tastes. They have a sub-teen daughter and an independent Siamese cat. Their interests run to music and books—and quiet entertaining for their circle of friends. Collecting American antiques is a greatly enjoyed hobby which the whole family shares.

Their furniture requirements for their home include the following: invitingly soft seating pieces, cabinets to house their collections and books, a desk for occasional correspondence, a chest for cover-up storage, and an organ for family music.

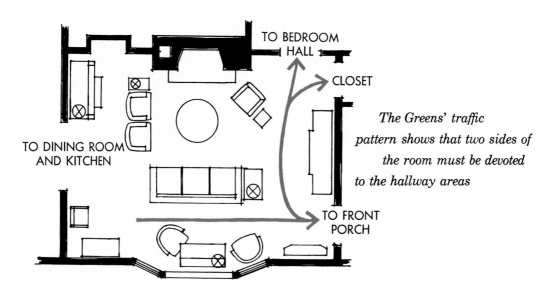

The Greens' traffic pattern shows that two sides of the room must be devoted to the hallway areas

1   This is the empty shell. Room-size rug appears brighter than it will when other furnishings are added—separates living areas from traffic "hallways."

2   The fireplace is the room's center of interest, so the major seating group is placed to emphasize it. Traffic passes around group without disturbing conversation.

Accents and accessories complete

the room scheme

Although of good size, the room is cut by the necessary traffic patterns into hallway areas on two sides. Planning on paper indicated this left only the center of the room available for the major conversational grouping, and limited both the number of side chairs and their size.

It also showed that the Greens would have to install an electric outlet in the floor to serve the sofa lamp, prevent tripping over cords.

Keep the theme

Now comes the fun of making this room "belong" to the Greens. Since their consuming interest is in the furnishings of Colonial America, their collections set the style for accessories and accents. Some pieces, such as the lamps, are modern, scaled to today's living, but follow the decorating theme in period design.

Conversation is easy

The sofa and chair grouping is compact, allows for easy conversation. Round coffee table serves both the sofa and one chair, while other chairs have their own tables, properly scaled, conveniently placed.

3 Old and new combine in a mellow scheme

The final, personal touch of accents and accessories turns this room into a warm and friendly place. The furniture i new, most of the accessories are old . . the feeling conveyed is one of conserva tive good taste.

The handsome breakfront gives need ed height, serves as an accent in itself picks up white from chairs and walls Its plus is hidden storage and displa space for treasured heirlooms and books. Accessories on top break the too straight line of door and cabinet.

Warmth, charm— good combination

Here's the view of the other side of the Green's living room, looking from the fireplace toward the bay window. Traffic passes behind the sofa, leaving family and friends in comfort. Organ, located on wall behind chairs, is out of the traffic path.

4 *The Greens take joy in traditional designs —coupled with sparkling contemporary color*

Here's the charm of Colonial design, plus the advantages of modern materials. White chairs are practical with today's dust- and stain-resistant finishes. Contemporary rugs, in any color, hold their hues, are available permanently mothproofed or in miraculous man-made fibers. Paint on light walls, shutters is scrubbable. Hunt chairs wipe off—can be pulled into conversation grouping for guests.

The Whites live in this traditional home

Planned for entertaining guests

The White family lives in a digni-fied, traditionally Eighteenth Century home. Their decor, based on the past, is successfully combined with the contemporary, open-plan of the living-dining-game area.

They have a teen-age daughter, a son just a bit younger, and a lovable and active dachshund. Grownups and children alike enjoy watching television, listening to the record collection, and playing cards. Their congenial living habits are reflected in their hospitable furnishings.

The Whites' furnishing requirements include comfortable chairs and a sofa, good lighting, plus plenty of pull-up seating for parties.

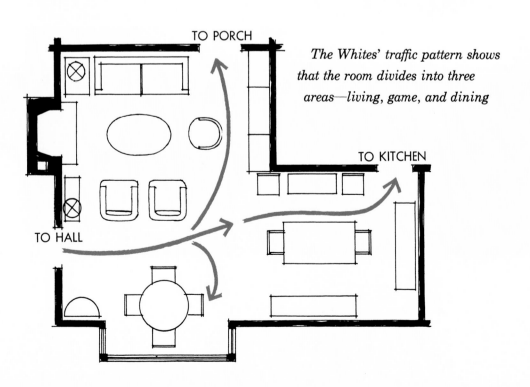

The Whites' traffic pattern shows that the room divides into three areas—living, game, and dining

TO PORCH

TO KITCHEN

TO HALL

1 Sofa fabric sets the color theme. Wall color, chair upholstery, carpet tones all stem from it. Wall-to-wall carpeting helps to unify the three activity areas.

2 The fireplace is the center of interest in the living-room section. Television and record-player are part of the bookcase grouping shown on the floor plan left.

Distinctive accessories retain a

classic feeling

The main seating group takes care of six people comfortably. Instead of buying chairs separately for the dining room and card table groupings, the Whites chose eight alike, scaled to fit with living room area furniture.

These eight additional chairs serve for dinner parties, for card games, or pull into the living room area. Each part of the room lives its own life, but interchanges furniture whenever it's necessary.

Accessories repeat basic color plan

Most of the accessories in the room repeat the basic colors in the sofa . . . blue, green, white . . . in varying shades and textures. Sparkle comes from the rich notes of gold and brass, with a sprinkling of deep red in flowers, fruits, bookbindings.

The formality of the room permits the combination of Eighteenth Century and elegant Provincial styling. Its accessories draw heavily on both periods, some with classic inspiration, some derived from spirited French or courtly British sources.

3 *Accessories contribute to graciousness of setting*

Dignified yet warm, well-chosen accessories have turned this room into a pleasant center of living for all the family and their friends. Modern materials make these light colors practical, even at a teen-age party.

The lamps are well-proportioned, placed to give adequate reading light. Crystal chandelier illuminates dining area. The coffee table serves the entire conversational group, is placed for convenience, yet far enough away from each seat so there's plenty of legroom, traffic can move about.

4 *Wallpaper mural reflects colors from the scheme*

Mural over the buffet adds pattern and variety, repeats both the basic colors of this decorating scheme, and the elegant note of its period furnishings . . . ties the two areas together without monotony.

The combination of low game table and vertical lines of the drapery trimming emphasize the height of the room.

Entertaining's a pleasure

5 *Furniture arrangement adds versatility to three areas*

Now the Whites have furnished to serve all three of the room's purposes; living, dining, and entertaining. And there's the plus of versatility. Game table can be used for pleasant, private breakfasts with a sparkling morning view. It doubles as a serving table for appetizers and drinks. It's also a pleasant place to work on hobbies apart from conversation, yet is close enough to be part of the group. Chairs serve either the dining or the living room areas.

Here's the other side of the room, which shows the dining area and the game center. The Whites love parties, so have chosen their furnishings to facilitate party giving. The accessories and accents here have been carefully selected, too . . . can trade places with those in the living area for variety . . . can be used for serving at any kind of a festive affair.

The Smiths look for comfort, informality in

Smart Contemporary design

The Smith family lives in a good-size contemporary ranch-style home, which reflects their love for informal comfort, indoor-outdoor living, and entertaining. They have a school-age son, delight in their talking bird.

They're interested in the sleek lines of today's designs, in Modern art, in flowers, books, music . . . are apt to adopt interesting hobbies such as weaving and ceramics.

They require comfort plus good design in their furnishings, plenty of storage room, and modern materials that require an absolute minimum of care. They need plenty of seating space, little formal dining space.

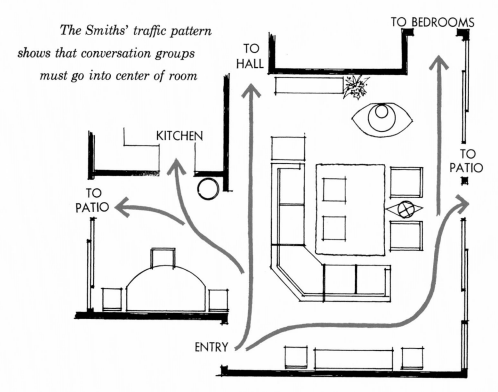

The Smiths' traffic pattern shows that conversation groups must go into center of room

TO BEDROOMS

TO HALL

KITCHEN

TO PATIO

TO PATIO

ENTRY

1 This is the background for their furnishings. The color of the rich woods and resilient flooring could be too somber, so needs brightening, depth of texture.

2 Terrace view and fireplace combine as a center of interest. Major seating is arranged to emphasize it. Light upholstery is practical with modern finishes.

Interplay of texture contributes

The Smiths have an eye for the dramatic—but avoid flamboyancy with knowledgeable use of texture, form.

Shining surfaces such as the oversize brass vase for the flowers, the enameled freestanding fireplace and smooth-surface flooring—these contrast with the shagginess of the rug, the softer texture of the sectional upholstery. The over-all color scheme derives from the rug, with its basic browns, beiges, touch of orange and yellow, a minute speck of off-white.

On the practical side, there are electric floor outlets for the table lamps at each end of the sofa and between yellow pull-up chairs which eliminate trailing extension cords.

A three-way hanging fixture serves the middle of the sofa, adds to the general illumination in the room.

Decorative panels are installed as sliding doors on the wall cabinet— beautiful as well as useful.

3 A minimum of clutter makes cleaning easy

Busy days for this family include chauffeuring on Mother's part . . . to school, to the train, to dancing classes . . . to the store—early into town, later returning for Father—and, the meandering projects of any small boy. There are exciting books to read, a houseful of company several times a week.

So this home is designed for an absolute minimum of time spent on housework. Easy-care materials, flexible furniture arrangement, plus a lack of clutter do the trick.

Current work and hobby projects are concealed in ample storage space, are brought out whenever convenient.

to over-all good design

The Smiths furnish for maximum flexibility

Here is a view of the Smiths' dining area, seen from the terrace entrance. Because they dine and entertain informally in both the dining area and the living room, the dining room furniture is planned for use with their other Contemporary furnishings.

Chairs are selected to blend with living room pieces, can be used for extra guest seating. The seat covers repeat the yellow accent note.

The table moves easily into the living room for handy service at parties. Grouping is placed against the wall, to free traffic path from kitchen to patio to living room.

4 Dining area is planned to serve four functions

Informal living frees dining area for use as a multipurpose room. Although small, it serves these functions:

1. As a study, there is shelf space for reference books, table top for work. Typewriter stores in cabinets on opposite side of room.

2. As a buffet area, it has good traffic circulation at parties.

3. As a serving area fo the private dining patio, it keeps foods unwilted and fresh indoors.

4. As a breakfast room, grouping need not be moved, is handy to kitchen.

The Browns are proud of their first home but

Consider a move in the future

The Brown family lives in its first home—small, but well planned for family enjoyment. They have an c-tive young son and an equally active young puppy. They favor Contemporary architecture and furniture, and bright modern colors.

Their furnishings are planned for present comfort and for use in a larger home in the future. A major requirement of the furniture is that it be easy to take care of while Baby is growing up. Another need is a desk which Father can use for his reports, and Mother for household bookkeeping and for family letter writing.

Because they will probably need a different arrangement in their next home—and wished to invest in immediate comfort—they chose a sectional, which will fit into almost any size room. Covers are removable for easy cleaning, and quick change.

The Browns' traffic pattern shows that this room can be divided into both living and dining areas

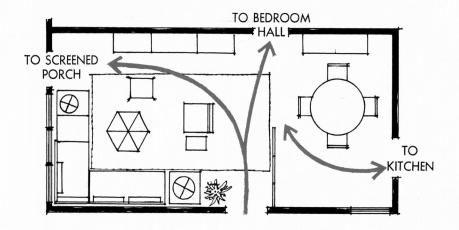

TO BEDROOM
HALL

TO SCREENED
PORCH

TO
KITCHEN

1 The vibrant color scheme derives from the panels of ready-made draperies—flexible, too, in the next home. Resilient flooring, room-size rug, are easy to clean.

2 Centers of interest are big window and storage-study wall. Sectional makes the most of both. Coffee table separates into pull-up tables for party entertaining.

Bright accents and accessories

reflect their modern tastes

Just what the Browns asked for—from the hard-surfaced flooring to the washable draperies and sofa slip covers—a room requiring a minimum of care from a busy young mother.

The furniture is arranged so that six people can be seated comfortably in a conversation group—and the sofa can double as an emergency guest bed. Cushions and dining room chairs pull in for a more crowded, but equally effective party arrangement.

Planned for the future

In addition, this furniture is of quality that will last, of design that will go into the Browns' next home with a minimum of fitting. The two sofa sections can each be used as a separate love seat, the matching bench can serve as a footstool, or, with a cushion, as extra seating. Coffee table converts to individual tables.

3 Accents and accessories offer a texture change

Major accessories here pick up the gleam of smooth texture, with polished brass, porcelain, and glass giving light, airiness to a colorful scheme.

Arrangement of accessories is important, too. Notice how the hanging light fixture becomes part of the table grouping, with a simple wood sculpture relating it to the table surface.

Both hanging light and table lamp are properly placed and in scale with table tops and seating arrangement.

Plants, flowers, and the picture with its powerful movement, add grace to the room, keep its sharp lines from seeming too stark.

4 Dining area is integral part

The kitchen is too small for an eating area, so the living room must serve this function, too. With a baby, it's easier to have a table and chairs set up at all times.

One end of the room is set aside for the dining area, screened from the living section by translucent panels which admit light, give a feeling of space.

Table will serve four, can go into a bigger home as a game table. Chairs pull into living room for guests.

5 Traffic path calls for wall-hung desk and storage units

Any furnishings on the long wall must free a traffic path between the dining room, hall, and porch. Here, hanging units free the floor, provide storage, and make a handsome center of interest. One unit is a desk with a pulldown front . . . can be used with a dining chair. Shelves hold both books and accessories.

chapter 5

Backgrounds
set the mood

Can you plan a background? Can you use pattern
on the ceiling? Can you have contrasting
woodwork? Can you combine bold pattern with
bright color? Yes—these 28 pages tell you how

Plan backgrounds to complement furnishings

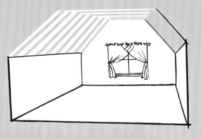

Pattern a ceiling?

Yes, if you want to lower a too-high ceiling, or call attention to an unusual shape

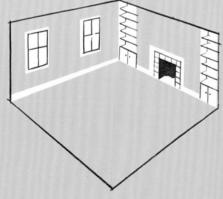

Use borders, dadoes?

Yes, to give a touch of vivid color and definite pattern, or a design to set a color theme

Use contrasting trim?

Yes, to emphasize beautiful moldings, built-ins, or to modify the size of a room that looks too big

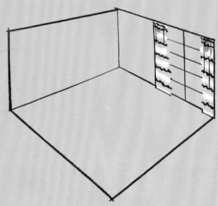

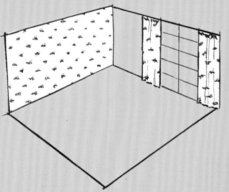

Plain colored walls?

Yes, particularly if you have a bold, dominating print in your upholstery or drapery fabrics

Companion patterns?

Yes, fabric and wallpaper that are printed alike can be used to balance pattern around a room

Decorate

six walls

Visualize the room you are decorating as a cube with four walls, a floor, and a ceiling as a background for furnishings. Draperies, striped in blue and green, paneling, sea-toned carpeting, beamed off-white ceiling encircle colorful furniture accents.

Pattern enlivens a ceiling

If you want to liven up an otherwise dull room, make it a little different, a good trick is to put major pattern and color on the ceiling. This is particularly effective if the ceiling is sloping or arched, or some other unusual shape, or if there's a dormer window in the room.

There are two methods of treating any space which is prominent or different, such as sloping or arched ceilings. One is to disguise it as much as possible. The other is to feature it. A small-patterned paper, also brought down to cover the walls, does a good disguise job. This treatment tends to hide jogs and imperfections. Or, the ceiling can be the focal point, emphasized with strong color and definite pattern in wallpaper.

Balance pattern, plain color

If you do make the ceiling a center of interest, balance the color and pattern with substantial areas of solid, strong color at floor level. Choose one or two of the solid colors from the paper for your upholstery and drapery materials.

A formal pattern sets off a traditional room

Wood paneling provides the background for this traditional room, but needs large areas of color and pattern to emphasize it. A formal wallpaper pattern in red with white accent details the beamed ceiling. Red and white are picked up from the paper for the upholstery fabrics and the cafe curtains.

Stripes pattern this game room ceiling

Pastel stripes create a circus-tent atmosphere in this rejuvenated recreation room. Draperies of matching fabric repeat the stripes at the windows without adding any other color or pattern. Seats of the ice-cream parlor chairs are painted in solid colors picked up from the circus-stripe.

WOOD PANELING IS STAINED TO BLEND WITH WALLS AND DRAPERIES

Pattern accents monochromatic backgrounds

When you use bold pattern in a room, you will probably want a softer, one-color background against which to display it. Color breaks between walls and woodwork are sharp, and call attention to the division.

Yet, if your room is a large one, with simple, clean lines, walls and woodwork painted alike can seem cold and lifeless. One way to achieve

WALLS AND CEILING OF A MATCHING TINT SURROUND FURNISHINGS

this one-color background look with an added touch of texture is to stain moldings and the paneling to blend and harmonize with your paint color.

Design a color shell

In designing a color shell for any room, remember that there are six big surfaces to consider—the floor, walls, and ceiling. Since you want the ceiling to be light in tone, to reflect a glow over all your furnishings, either paint it lighter than the walls, or have both walls and ceiling in a clear, light tint. If you use the same color for your floor covering, be sure it's deeper in tone than walls and ceiling. This will give an appearance of weight at the floor level.

Matching woodwork creates harmony within room, imparts spacious feeling

Small rooms look much larger Panels, doors of varied tones would have made this room look crowded. Instead, a single color unites dado, fireplace wall, and woodwork.

Cut-up room looks uncluttered

The same crisp colors, carried from one room to another, give this home its serene, cozy look. Louvered shutters are painted to match.

Modern architecture emphasizes use

FIREPLACE WALL IS CENTER OF INTEREST, BLENDS WITH THE WOOD COLORS

# of natural materials for walls

USE EARTH TONES FOR WARMTH

There's a trend in architecture —toward bringing the outdoors inside as part of your decorating scheme, letting the natural beauty of trees, grass, and sky complement the interior. And the indoors, in its turn, serves as a frame —for the lovely view you incorporated when building.

As a result, the unadorned natural materials used in building are often used in interior decorating, as well as for the exterior of the home. In addition to being handsome, such materials as brick and stone, siding, and paneling have the great advantage of being easy to care for.

Copy natural materials

For those who live in older homes, but are remodeling and rejuvenating the rooms, there are many copies of these natural materials that will give the desired effect— effects that will add new life to interiors.

Marbleized patterns come in many colors. In addition there are papers that resemble silver-gray weathered boards or highly polished knotty-pine paneling. Some papers are even three dimensional—with the individual bricks or pieces of stone jutting out, making handy ledges.

Real woods that have been shaved in thin sheets and mounted on a paper or canvas back, can be put on the walls as easily as paper.

Painted panels add color punch,

It's a basic premise of color-styling that pale colors seem to push walls away, increase the feeling of space. They're particularly valuable when you decorate compact rooms.

Bright colors can also enlarge

Bright colors, used with finesse and skill, along with the paler tones, can add to the sensation of space, too.

The framework of the room should utilize the lighter colors. But within this framework, at the end of a hallway, showing through a door, defining the end of a room, sharp color beckons the eye, leads it to a visually distant point.

Blend brightness with accents

When you use these bright panels of color as an eye-teaser, repeat their tones in the same or another value elsewhere in the room. Let them serve as underscoring for the accent and accessory colors you've selected to go with your basic color scheme. The general background color should be light, to emphasize space, furniture tones deep and natural.

Colorful panels, framed in white, draw eye outward

An open floor plan gives an illusion of space here, greatly helped by pale color on floor and in draperies.

The sharp accent colors of orange and yellow, framed in white, emphasize the far end of the room, first on the divider wall, then more brilliantly in the orange of the dining area panel.

spaciousness to multipurpose room

Paint changes a room

There's nothing like a new background color to give your tired-looking rooms a new lease on life. A new paint color changes the whole feeling of your home. If your colors are all blended with one another, try contrasting tones.

If the walls have been dark in the past, change their color to a soft pastel. Color is *your* choice, but be sure it complements the furnishings you already have. Select a tone from your drapery fabric, or a light blending of your floor covering.

By selecting from one of the paint manufacturers' color systems, it is easy to find just the tone you want.

Color changes size, too

A lighter tone can make your rooms look larger. A darker color can pull the walls closer. Select colors to absorb light if the room is too sunny— even if it is small. Choose tones to reflect light if the room is dark, and plan to add lamps and fixtures to enhance the color plan.

If you like dark colors,
select a brighter tone

The green of these walls was selected from the mat of the picture over the fireplace. It gives an unusual effect of a double frame. With a bright, deep shade like this, it is a good idea to paint the fireplace to exactly match.

If you like medium-bright colors, choose a warm tone

What a different feeling the warm cocoa of these walls gives. The tone goes well with the cherry tables, picks up the brown of the lounge-chair pattern. White fireplace and light, bright accessories give the contrast needed.

If you like lighter colors, pick to blend

The soft ivory walls blend with the beige rug, the honey tones of accessories, and sofa, make the room seem larger than it really is.

A pastel rose to blend with the cushions on the sofa would have been an equally good choice. A green to pick up the color of the picture mat would also be effective.

A STYLIZED WALLPAPER TREE SETS SIMPLE COLOR SCHEME

PATTERN IS REPEATED ON THIS WALL WITH CUTOUT BRANCHES

Study the basic pattern types

Pattern and color combined can do many things—camouflage architectural mistakes, cover up protruding beams and jogs in walls, make a room seem higher, or push out the walls to give more apparent space. There are big patterns and little ones, bright colors and subtle ones. Each has its place in your decorating scheme.

There are ten basic types of wallpaper patterns from which to choose: *trompe l'oeil*, or "fool-the-eye"; the all-over pattern; the small pattern; the large pattern; the background pattern; textured pattern; copies of architectural materials; scenics, murals; borders and dadoes.

No matter what your style of decorating is, or the kind of furniture you have—Traditional or Contemporary —Colonial or Provincial—there is a pattern in one of these categories that can brighten your home.

What's the problem

Take a good, close look, find your decorating problem. Is the room too small, too low—too long, or too wide? Pattern, color will help solve it.

"Fool-the-eye" adds space

If you like a feeling of space, but live in tiny rooms, try one of the *trompe l'oeil* wallpaper patterns. It could be a mountain scene, or a garden, or a pleasant countryside—all designed to carry the eye out and away from the enclosing four walls.

These papers also come in scenic murals, with strips to be joined together, or they are available in regular rolls—like the snowy view seen through a mullioned window, at the left.

Allover patterns unify room

Do you want to camouflage the sloping line of a ceiling—or make a jog in the wall look straight? Then try an allover wallpaper pattern. Be sure it is nondirectional, that is—that the pattern looks the same from any angle or any view.

Many allover wallpaper patterns come with a matching fabric for draperies or upholstery. If you use both, be sure that all the other decorating elements in the room are in solid colors—let the print be the one dominant pattern.

A small pattern adds interest

The difference between an allover pattern and a small pattern is just this—the former is nondirectional, the latter has a definite up-and-down or across direction.

The small pattern is a good choice in a room where you want color and neat symmetry, without the disturbance of bold figure—in a room where quietness is desired, such as a bedroom or a study-guest room.

The tiny pattern illustrated at the left reaches upward, gives height without distraction.

Textured patterns give variety

"Texture" means that the pattern has a three-dimensional look, as if it were woven of threads or fibers. These textures are usually found in neutral tones, give variety without adding color or pattern. Typical designs are simulated woven blinds, grass cloth.

Some copy natural materials

Contemporary architecture emphasizes the use of natural materials for interior walls—just as did the home designs of Colonial America. Brick or stone, marble, marquetry, or fine paneling—any of these can be yours with an investment in a few rolls of wallpaper.

Definite patterns set the theme

When each design is a separate and distinct decorative motif, then it is called "definite." This kind of pattern is almost always used as the basis for the color scheme, as the dominant feature of the room. Flowers, abstracts, and stripes are members of this family.

Patterns serve as backgrounds

Do you like pattern and color on your walls—and pictures, too? Then select a wallpaper design from the "background" family. These are small motifs, spaced far enough apart so that they will not draw attention from any wall accessories you may want to use.

Borders, dadoes act as accents

If you'd like a touch of vivid color and definite pattern, try a gay wallpaper border. They are especially useful in kitchen, bath, or Baby's room, where wall surfaces need to be scrubbable. Architectural dadoes in paper give elegant accent to ordinary rooms.

Large patterns give character

Give your rooms character, and a decorative center of interest, with an extra large pattern, perhaps on only one wall. Choose it to blend with your furnishings style, to add interest to the central scheme. In this room, a stylized hanging lantern sets the Oriental theme.

Murals and scenics dress up a room

In addition to the nine basic wallpaper types already illustrated, there is another major category which adds special beauty to walls.

This is the mural and scenic design. A mural is a picture executed on a wall. A scenic is a mural that depicts a scene of some sort, usually a landscape, in contrast to abstract or floral designs.

Usually sized to fit an entire wall, they can be hung above a dado—or used as a focal point above a server. Matching plain paper is usually available for use on other walls.

Mural adds architectural significance to an ordinary room

The furnishings are restrained, architecturally simple in design. They need a touch of dramatic boldness . . . one unifying element is necessary. The bare walls need dressing up, a touch of elegance added. Here, a wall mural does the job. It's more than just an abstract picture—it's a sweep of design that enhances both the architectural design of the room and its contemporary feeling.

Murals have many decorative uses. Of course, you wouldn't want one on every wall—there would be no place left for the furniture. But one wall-wide picture can be the dramatic focus of all your decorating.

A mural can be the basis for the style used in your decorating. If your home is contemporary, select one of the stylized modern designs that are available. If your home is traditional, your choice might be a rustic country scene, or an adaptation of a city view during colonial times, as sketched below.

Remember, a mural *is* a picture, and a dominating one. You won't want to use another big picture or grouping which would compete.

A mural also gives you a ready-made color scheme to copy, as shown on pages 90-99. Study the mural—get acquainted with the colors and the amounts in which they're used.

A shade of the dominant color could be used on other walls, or in the floor-covering. Secondary tones would provide color for upholstery and drapery fabrics. Bright accents would appear in the accessories.

An airy scenic pushes out the walls of a tiny room

Look out to loveliness, to generous space—highlight your decorating with a scenic mural. Here, small windows are curtained to give light and air, while the "view" is concentrated on one wall. Most scenics fit easily in the available space. And most are designed so that each panel is a picture in itself. If your space is really limited, use only two or three panels, instead of the set.

Matching prints solve decorating problems

If you have a too-small room and still want lots of color and pattern . . . or if your room has many architectural faults you want to hide . . . or if you just can't decide on curtains or draperies, consider using a patterned wall covering and fabric to match.

From a Colonial living room to a starkly Contemporary den, from a cozy family room to a party room, you'll find a pattern in matching paper and fabric that will dress it up. A small pattern is usually more satisfactory where you have jogs and turns to hide. If you use it on a ceiling, too, be sure the pattern is nondirectional, can be used in any position.

A big pattern in matching paper and fabric can set a decorating theme, and is most often used in a playroom, or a family or game room.

Used with discretion, these matching papers and fabrics take care of half a dozen decorating problems all at the same time.

Small patterns hide jogs

Dress walls and windows alike to tie together a room with many jogs, windows, and doors. Here, the tiny pattern unifies the background. Pattern makes ceiling look lower.

A gay hobby pattern sets the theme for a family room

Even a small room can take a big pattern when it is used with discretion. Here all the pattern and the movement is concentrated on the walls. Carpet and upholstery tones blend with the pattern background, as do the wood tones of the other furniture. Pattern at the windows only or on the walls only would have looked spotty here, made the room seem smaller. In effect, pattern as used here actually becomes only a background, not the dominant force in the room's color scheme.

Co-ordinate with related prints

When you want to vary your pattern without destroying its effect, or carry the pattern into another room in a different way . . . consider using some of the new companion papers.

A pattern should always be repeated somewhere in a room for balance, but sometimes it is so bold that it is difficult to do so without making two centers of interest. That's the time to use companion papers, which are two or more separate patterns, designed to be used together. Usually one is a big, bold print, the other repeating a small motif or a textured background from the big one. These papers also help to carry your decorating theme from one room to another without monotony, with the big print used in hall or dining room, the small one as a background for the living room furnishings.

Use the same pattern with a different background color

Try this trick if you can't find companion papers you like. The entry and stairway halls here are both papered in the same pattern, with different colored backgrounds. The theme is carried on into the living room with a fabric matching the entry-hall paper used for slip covers. Painted walls and draperies blend with a pale green note in the wallpaper pattern, further correlate color between the rooms.

A tiny companion print can be used on a broken wall

A stylized pattern of little fishes swimming through nets and seines strikes an almost architectural note in this contemporary home. The companion paper of the little fishes alone is small enough and abstract enough to be used on the closet wall without being interfered with by the pattern of the closet doors. Notice how the main theme is printed so that it can be adjusted to walls of varying height.

Wallpaper in special patterns

sets a mood

There are innumerable delightful wallpaper patterns that can express your family's interests, hobbies. From the papers available, you can select background and accent colors that will give personality to your home. Give emphasis to the pattern by using it sparingly—on a long wall or on a floor-to-ceiling screen.

Maybe you're a weekend sailor, or a frustrated wanderer, or are owned by a puppy, a kitten, or even a goldfish. You like bridge—or golf—or tennis. Then make your selection from one of the many wallpapers that illustrate your interests.

Select soft background tones

Because you'll want to feature the special pattern of the paper, select soft tones for other walls, woodwork, and floor covering. This will make your bright pattern stand out. Choose a deeper tone of the plain wall color or the carpeting for the major upholstered pieces. Then add just one— or two at the most—of the brightest colors in the form of accents, such as ash trays, pillows, lamp bases or shades.

Keep accessories simple

Because a special pattern is likely to be bold in scale, color, and form, you do not want any other definite patterns to distract attention from it. So keep your decorative objects few and very simple, clean in line, without added decoration.

A love of Naval history prompted this simple color scheme

The history of wooden ships and iron men reflects a hobby in this home. Neutral tones of carpeting, draperies, enhance the deep-water-blue spread and the pale blue walls.

Accessory colors stand out

against a pale background

Intense colors glow against walls that blend with the backgrounds of two exciting paintings. Non-reflective glass protects them. Woven-to-order rug picks up the painting colors. Copy the idea by sewing together inexpensive strips of carpeting.

chapter 6

Glamorize your floors

Your floors often set the pace of your

room. Consider some of the new finishes

new colors . . . new patterns . . . new shapes . . .

new sizes . . . new materials

Pages 187 through 204

Choose from the six basic types

Use area rugs as dividers

Area rugs are those smaller rugs—square, oval, round, oblong, or free-form—that define and set aside one living area from another in the same room. Be sure that they are large enough so that at least part of the piece of furniture sits on the rug. Otherwise the group may look skimpy

Wall-to-wall enlarges rooms

If your room is too small, or cut-up, the unbroken sweep of color you get in wall-to-wall carpeting will make it look larger, less cluttered. There is no sharp break to stop the eye. It's easy to care for, too—just a vacuuming will take care of whole job, without back-breaking mopping

Room-size rugs are easy to fit

"Room-size" is the name given to the standard 6, 9, 12 and 15-foot wide rugs you can buy cut and bound, ready to put down on floors. They come in almost any imaginable length to fit your rooms. Purchase these rugs in sizes to show as little floor space around the outside edges as possible

New beauty in hard-surface

There are three common hard-surface floorings to consider in decorating, in addition to the more exotic ones. One is natural wood in long boards or parquetry. The other two are tile squares and yard-goods in linoleum, vinyls, cork, rubber, asphalt. All come in decorative colors

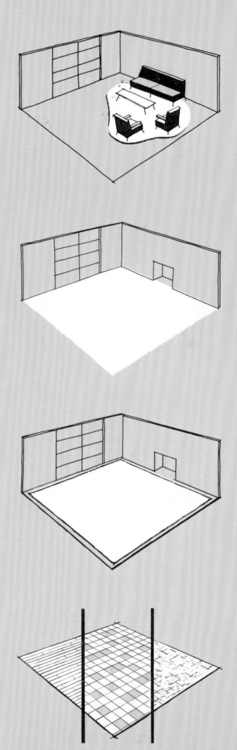

Color stems
from the floor

Truly—there is "glamour underfoot" with this dramatic contemporary carpet setting the room's color theme. Deep-brown background underscores pale brick and painted walls, soft beige and cocoa chairs and light woods, and is echoed in the sofa print and dark mahogany step tables. The sharp blue is repeated in coffee table, chair.

Color—pattern—texture

A textured blend of color suits an informal room

A contemporary carpet adaptation of the old rag rug gives texture underfoot in an informal room, is equally compatible with Traditional or Modern furnishings. Tone-on-tone effects, carved, other three-dimensional motifs, patterns, florals or geometrics, can be found to suit any decor.

Glowing color, a deep pile, set a decorating theme

True color in today's dyes, whether for synthetics or natural fibers, gives lasting beauty to floor coverings. Here, a popular blue-green is repeated in bedspreads and headboards, echoed in a tone of the plaid which accents the dominant color.

Wool . . . cotton . . . synthetics . . . blends of natural fibers and test-tube beauties—there's almost unlimited choice for every use, every purse. Warmth, color, and softness underfoot, are available now for every home in any price range.

Jewellike colors inspire fresh, new schemes, rug patterns dominate your room. Today's dyes are true and clear, keep their beauty for the life of the rug. New weaves and fibers simplify cleaning. Natural fibers come permanently mothproofed.

If your floor covering contains more than one fiber, the major one determines the cleaning process.

Whatever your choice of rug or carpet, don't economize on the cushioning. A top-quality cushion doubles the life of a floor covering. It protects fibers against shock of repeated footsteps, fills in uneven spaces of floor that might cause worn spots.

Rugs, carpets inspire good color schemes

If you have a patterned rug or carpet, the procedure for developing a color scheme from it is the same as for developing one from any other pattern such as patterned fabric or wallpaper.

First, select from the design that tone or shade which you want to use for a background. You don't have to match it exactly, but rather blend it. You know that color in quantity becomes more intense. So, for instance, if your favorite in the rug pattern is a rather strong blue, chances are that it would be too bright to use in quantity on your walls. So you "gray" it, or subdue it a little, but keep the same color value. Or you may prefer a blending color halfway between two of the pattern tones—such as a pale olive-green to blend with beige and green.

Second, select one, two, or three stronger colors for major upholstered pieces. If your carpet or rug pattern is a many-colored one, a floral, or a complicated Oriental design, you will probably be more satisfied with only one or two. You would not want to introduce another definite pattern into the upholstery fabrics, but you could well choose one in a subtle stripe that combines both background and secondary colors.

Third, choose one or two still brighter tones and use them as accent colors—in lamp shades, in pillows, in small upholstered pieces, in pottery, in ash trays, and boxes.

Keep patterns subdued in all three of these steps, so that the rug remains dominant.

The color, formality, and pattern of an Oriental rug set the theme here

Deep cafe au lait of the paper blends with wood trim, dado. Rose chair, blue accessories, pictures, repeat a rug tone. Blue walls, carpeting, draperies in adjoining room also stem from rug colors.

Wall-to-wall carpeting or room-size rug?

What's your choice—wall-to-wall carpeting or a room-size rug? Both types have their advantages.

As a decorative element, carpeting gives an uninterrupted sweep of fresh color from wall to wall.

Carpeting makes a small room look bigger

Vivid carpeting provides a continuous sweep of cheery color from wall to wall, visually enlarges this small den-guest room. Slip covers, draperies pick up floor color, combine with blue walls in a crisp color scheme.

Select room-size rugs that fit the area

No matter what the shape or size of a room, carpeting fits around all the corners, with no unsightly gaps.

Rugs come in standard widths and lengths—6x9, 9x12, 12x15, or any length necessary may be cut to order from standard carpeting rolls. Allow about six inches of floor to show on all sides. In selecting a rug, an obvious advantage is its mobility. It's almost always possible to find a place for a rug, even in a new home.

This room-size rug exposes a minimum of floor around the edges. Its heavy, three-dimensional weave gives the depth and texture contrast needed against all the smooth surfaces in the room. A rug is a dividend for a family room— it can be rolled to one end of the room for parties, teen-age dancing.

Area rugs
define space
with color

An "area" rug is one which separates one area of a room from another, divides living spaces. Furniture of any particular grouping should either be completely *on* rug, or completely *off*—never half and half·

Consider scatter rugs, too—small rugs up to 4x6 feet, used wherever you need a spot of warmth or color, usually next to a bed, near a door.

Standard-size rugs
set a basic color theme

A good plan for anyone, but particularly valuable to families that must move often, is a group of matching rugs. As the basis for the color scheme, they will move smoothly into any home. In a big, open-plan room like this, they also define various living areas.

Bold pattern of the area rug →
emphasizes parquet flooring

Here, the furniture is grouped *around* the rug—a strong focal point which highlights the handsome flooring.

The pattern is the only one in the room, with all other colors drawn from it, or blending with it. It's properly sized for the furniture grouping.

Select the right rug or carpet for each room

There are rugs or carpets suitable for living room, dining room, bedroom, hallway, bath—kitchen, guest room, study—anyplace where there's a need for softness, warmth, color.

There are soft velvety piles, twisted resilient yarns, three-dimensional effects in carved motifs, tweedlike textures, woven rugs of hard fibers. There are florals, stripes, muted colors blended subtly together, brilliant jewel tones that keep fresh looking and lovely for all their years.

There are carpets and room-size rugs, scatter and area rugs.

Natural fibers are practical for a family room

Fiber squares sewed together are easy to brush clean, give interesting texture and variety to a monochromatic scheme. All tones are variations of basic golden brown. One-color look is a space-maker in a small room, because it helps disguise shapes, sizes.

Carpeting extends color up an open stairway

When an open stairway ascends from a hallway or living room, as shown here, carry the carpeting on up to the second floor, so that there'll be no break in the sweep of color from one level to another. Wall-to-wall carpeting will quiet clatter, help prevent accidents, too, with less danger of catching a heel on the stair risers.

Put a rug in the kitchen? Yes, it *is* a practical idea. A washable scatter rug in front of your sink is a good investment because its resiliency helps to keep you fresh and feeling good, even after hours on your feet. Keep two— one on the floor, toss the other into the laundry once a week. Choose to blend with your kitchen decorating theme, or to point up bright accents.

Carpet your bathroom? Yes, it *is* a practical idea, if it is of washable material. For a tiny investment you get a return of luxury and beauty. Cut a paper pattern of your bathroom floor, showing all the plumbing outlets there, and the outlines of the fixtures.

Transfer the pattern to the back of the carpeting you have chosen. A word of caution—be sure that the pattern is upside down, too! Otherwise you'll find your pattern reversed when you are finished, and the job spoiled. Then cut the carpet according to the pattern —with a straight line in from the nearest edge to holes you cut around washstands, and so on. Lay the finished carpet on the floor without fastening it down in any way. It will stay in place while in use, and can easily be taken up for washing.

Carpet a bedroom? Yes, it *is* practical. One vacuuming does the whole cleaning job in brief minutes.

Carpets and hard-surface flooring— a workable team

Even if you want the comfort and softness of carpets, there may be places where you need the special advantages of hard-surface flooring. Here are some ways to combine these materials. You can suggest walls and define living areas, make a garden space, as we illustrate here. If you have a folding door that separates two carpeted rooms, cut your carpeting and insert a strip of wooden floor

Curve carpet edges to separate living areas

In an open-plan home you can use carpeting to suggest walls and define areas. Note how it has been curved to make a transition between the slate-floored entranceway and the living room. This plan also helps to define traffic patterns, makes arrangement easier.

or inlaid material, so that the door rides on a hard surface.

When you choose your hard-surface floor, you'll find vinyls and cork, linoleum, asphalt, rubber in easy-to-lay tiles, or in by-the-yard lengths. Some can be installed on a concrete slab foundation, or in a basement. Other hard-surface floorings should have an airspace below the floor for the longest possible wear.

Hard-surface flooring makes crumb-sweeping easy

Here, the area under and around the dining table takes spilled foods in stride. The oval cutout wasn't wasted—it was used to good advantage in an upstairs hallway.

Leave an area of hard-surface flooring for plant arrangement

Bring your garden right into the house for year-round beauty—and with never a fear for dirty carpets and floors.

Instead of bringing the carpet all the way to the wall near the windows, a small area of hard-surface flooring is left exposed. It makes a sunny place to display plants with no worry about spilling or other messy gardening accidents.

Hard-surface floors give built-in color in your home

→

White tiles with blue dots dress up a playroom

Games and toys can't harm this floor—it's also clean with a quick wipe. The blue dot in the tile is picked up for banquette upholstery, repeated in the luncheon china pattern. A low lunch bar separates the playroom from the kitchen—makes it easy for Mother to supervise while going about her daily routine.

An allover pattern adds color to a family room

This is a room where the whole family can relax—with never a worry about housekeeping. Practical hard-surface tile in a soft, allover pattern sets the color theme. Beige background blends with wood paneling. Pink, lavender are picked up for upholstery, accented with black. Drapery pattern repeats all the colors.

RESILIENT CORK TILES BLEND WITH LIGHT WOODS IN THIS ROOM

SYNTHETIC COATING MAKES CORK PRACTICAL FOR EVERYDAY USE

Tiles pattern this hallway

Resilient tiles create simple pattern in this distinctive entrance hall, echo shoji-like pattern of the front doors. Smooth-surface flooring is a logical choice here—is easy to keep clean, defines the entrance area.

chapter 7

Wake up your home with
lighting

Good lighting is decorating's third dimension.

It's easy to plan lighting to make the most of

color and furniture arrangement. Here are 26

pages of illustrations, ideas, and suggestions

See better . . . see beauty

Light for better vision

The most important concept of good lighting is that it should help you see better. Place lamps, fixtures so that there is no glare to disturb, no dark areas to strain. At every chair should be a lamp that is high enough to cast a glow over reading material held in the lap. Survey your family's hobbies and habits. Plan specific lighting for children's study and play, for card playing, reading in bed, shaving and make-up, work, and sewing

Enjoy your decorating

You've spent hours in matching colors, in planning arrangements, in making your home more beautiful. Plan your lighting so that you can enjoy this beauty day or night. Balance your lighting so that every part of the room has the same cheerful glow—and arrange contrasts for drama. If your walls are dark, compensate with more and bigger lamps, brighter bulbs. Spotlight important accessories and wall decorations to make the most of them. Select materials under the same lighting by which they will be seen in the home

Provide high-key light for every chair

Be good to your eyes—and your decorating—with two-purpose light. Cornice or valance installations give a soft background. In limited space, try a traveling pulley light, which can be brought down at any point for direct illumination.

Plan for two-purpose lighting

Home lighting has two purposes—first, it should protect your eyes; second, it should enhance your decorating scheme.

To achieve these ends, every home should have illumination on two levels, or keys—high and low. The high key is specific light for a specific purpose—directed onto work, reading, study, or play, giving the right kind of light for the job being done. The low key is soft and general and lights the whole room.

Cornice or valance lighting, or a ceiling fixture, provide general illumination, while table, floor lamps, or pulldown fixtures, supply high key and special lighting needs.

Or, you can plan a dimming system that raises or lowers the intensity of light to suit any mood at the turn of a knob—even fluorescent lamps.

If you install a low-voltage, remote-control system, you can control any number of lights and appliances from one location in the house.

Good lighting is an essential

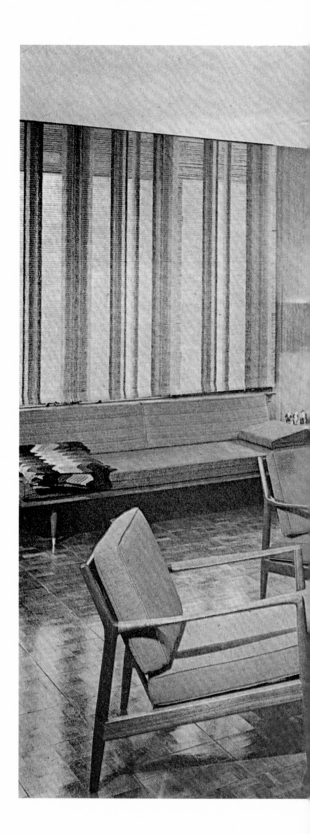

Lighting is the third element of good decorating . . . combined with comfortable and practical furniture arrangement, wise use of color, drapery and upholstery materials.

Take advantage of natural light to emphasize the beauty of your home . . . supplement it with artificial light so the colors glow at any time of day . . . under any kind of lighting conditions—sunny, dusky, or dark.

Combine natural, artificial

First, consider the angle of the light which comes through your windows. You've already planned arrangement of your furnishings to take advantage of natural light. Also, you've probably unconsciously considered natural light sources in choosing the arrangement of color in the room.

If you want to make the most of colors and shapes after dark, plan artificial lighting that comes from the same general direction.

In addition, you'll want general lighting, provided by cornice or valance fixtures, lamps for reading, perhaps dramatic spotlights to point up prized possessions.

Windows, fixtures offer

round-the-clock illumination

There are two major areas here . . . the grouping around the focal point of the fireplace, the leisure grouping on the window walls. In the latter, windows serve for daytime reading, a large corner lamp for evening, supplemented by a ceiling spot. Hanging lamps over the table highlight accessories.

part of decorating your home

Two-purpose light in your dining room

Soft enough to create a hospitable atmosphere, strong enough to bring out the beauty of table appointments, bright enough for expert serving—these are the lighting requirements for your dining room.

Good low-level illumination should flatter both diners and food . . . candles are sparkling, without being disturbing. Use high-level lighting on buffet or serving table, dramatize wall accessories with spotlights.

Decorative ceiling fixture supplements kitchen light

Since plenty of light comes in from the kitchen, this dining area needed a fixture that would give subtle light, plus being dramatic and decorative. Bullet lights on the wall can be turned to spot either the server, or to add to table brilliance.

Fixtures can provide
either kind of light

In a separate dining room, which will probably be used primarily after dark, you should provide both general and specific lighting. Here, a wall fixture illuminates the buffet, gives general glow to the room. Pulldown fixture concentrates on the table.

TABLE LAMP SERVES THE LOUNGE CHAIRS, SPOT ACCENTS ACCESSORIES

Two-purpose light in your bedroom

Don't underestimate the importance of two-purpose light in your bedrooms. Reading in bed is a pleasure most of us pursue—but be sure that the lighting is adequate. A small spot shining on a page is not good for the eyes. You need some general illumination, too. And be sure that the light from bedside lamps covers the reading page completely.

Decorative lighting is part of your plan, too, especially if the bedroom

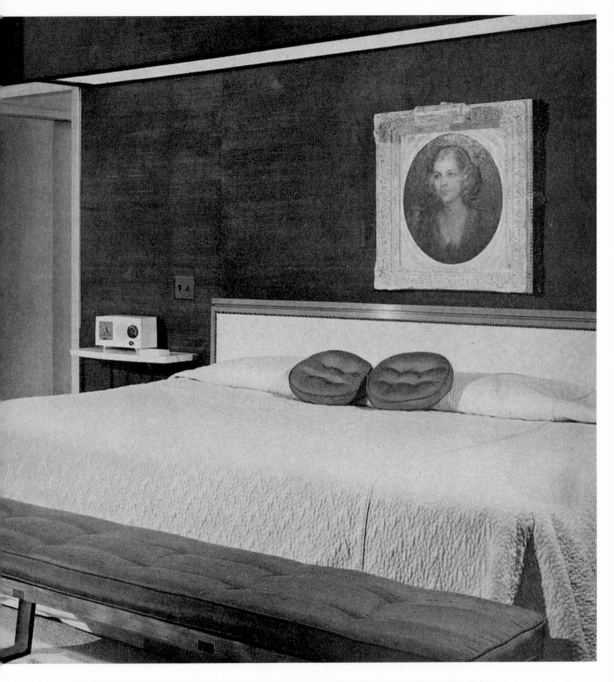

TROUGH LIGHTING OVER BED SERVES FOR GENERAL ILLUMINATION

doubles as a sitting room. Tranquil beauty is the keynote—plan for enough lighting to show it off.

Comfortable chairs, handy tables, well-placed reading lamps—these help to make the room an enchanting place to relax.

Balance your lighting

Remember the "rules" of using color —first, the background in a soft tone, then upholstery and drapery colors in a medium value, finally the sharp, bold accents.

The same principles hold true for lighting. First comes general, soft, over-all light, then brighter beams for working or reading. Then, point up your important accessories and accent pieces with dramatic spots.

The combination of these three light values will provide a perfect balance of light in any room.

Two-purpose light in your bathroom

Bathroom lighting should provide ample illumination for shaving and applying make-up. In these examples, reflected light from mirror and counter tops lights under-the-chin area to ensure a clean shave. By using a warm white bulb, you'll avoid distortion of make-up color.

Frosted ceiling panels reflect light in mirror

Ceiling panels diffuse the warm white light of fluorescent tubes into general, high-key lighting. Light-colored counter tops and the big mirror reflect light up and out, serve well for applying make-up and for shaving.

Ceiling spots light up shaving, make-up counter

Spots in the ceiling above each bowl are reflected from the mirror and the shiny, light-colored counter top. The mirror is set low, to reflect light under the chin for shaving. Side lighting fixtures would be an additional good light source.

Two-purpose light for children's work and play

Unless yours are the perfect little ladies and gentlemen who sit straight in their chairs, with neatly crossed ankles, book held in proper position and head high—you'll need to make special lighting provision for the children's bedrooms.

Most children play, study, or read on the floor, at a table or desk, or on the bed. So you will need high level, or directed, light on all three of these areas, plus the always-present, and essential general lighting.

For the desk, a good choice would be adjustable pin-up lamps against a light background, for good reflection. The reading light at the bedside could be a similar design, adjustable both sideways and up and down, to conform to the variations of little wrigglers. A floor lamp that can turn up or down could serve both a chair and the floor at playtime. All should have diffusing bowls.

Modern plastic lamps are very useful in children's rooms, because they resist breakage. And be sure that the bases of floor lamps are heavy and sturdy enough so that they are not easily overturned.

Consider special outlets

If your children are very small, and at the into-everything stage, consider the special lamp plug installations which prevent shock. Another idea is to put nursery plugs, wherever possible, high up on the walls.

←

Most important—

protect child's eyesight

Ceiling panels which give general lighting are made of white corrugated plastic set in flush below fluorescent tubes. They form a decorative note in a room, as well as a practical one.

Light from desk lamp is reflected onto work by the light wood behind it. Plan for efficiency first, good looks second. Remember, eyesaving results are most important for children.

→

Adjustable high-level

lights are practical

Just because children are so active, give them the kind of lamps and fixtures they can adjust to follow them when they change positions. You'll be rewarded with the best of eye protection.

Here, floor lamp turns down to the floor, up a little to serve the chair, straight up as a torchere for general lighting. Desk light pulls up or down, bed lights crisscross to any position.

Adequate lighting
is an aid to good vision

Round-the-clock lighting

Adequate lighting is especially important in decorating—you've spent hours in matching colors, so give those colors enough light to enjoy them. At night, let some of the principal lights come from about the same direction as the light did during the day.

Cove or valance illumination retains the luminous daytime look of window fabric and blinds. If you're in an older home, you probably need more circuits for laborsaving machines, so plan for eyesaving lighting, too. Talk it over with an expert—for safety's sake, wiring should be done by a professional.

Light rooms evenly

You're happier on a sunny day. And psychologists say a cheerfully lighted room gives the same emotional lift. The best for your spirits and your eyes, too, is fairly even lighting throughout a room, with extra lamps at special work areas. It's the spotty, uneven contrast of dark, shadowy corners and glaring illumination that overexercises eyes.

Your eye has a built-in exposure meter and automatic lens control that widens and narrows the lens opening to compensate for less or more light. Cooperate with the control by lighting evenly to avoid eyestrain.

Adjust light brilliance to color

Shiny and light-toned surfaces throw back the light, while dark surfaces soak it up. If you choose dark walls, plan to use more lamps and bigger, brighter bulbs. Keep the ceiling color light, so light will reflect. Average-size rooms need at least five lamps distributed around them, assuming there are pale walls and ceilings in the rooms.

Some ways to add light to a dark-walled room are by the use of mirrors, translucent shades or groupings of spotlights, as shown in drawing here.

Balance lighting for television

Television comfort requires balanced, all-around lighting as shown here. There is light coming from the tube almost ten times as bright as the reflected light on a movie screen, so your eyes need compensating light from other sources—but without a glare.

Good additions to the light from the screen are cove lighting or torcheres reflecting against a light-colored ceiling, or a lamp with a translucent shade. The latter is better for your eyes if it is not placed directly on the set.

Built-in light is convenient

Brighten up your storage shelves with built-in lighting, and add both beauty and convenience. Inside the phonograph you could add a light which turns on when you raise the lid. Or install such a light in the box where you store winter blankets and clothes.

If you're annoyed by a tangle of appliance cords around the night stand, "build" light into the stand so only one cord runs to the wall outlet. Use a "table tap" like an extension cord with a flattened double outlet.

Lighting enhances decorating

Locate outlets for use

Acquiring adequate wiring is the first step to decorating with light. Figure out *all* the appliances you want serviced, and *all* the light fixtures and lamps you will need. Then call in professional help to do the actual wiring job.

Conveniently placed outlets are next in importance. Temporary remedies are devices approved by Underwriters' Laboratories for carrying a cord along a baseboard. Metal strips with outlets at 1-foot intervals can be placed along baseboards or tops of work counters. Install floor outlets for "island" groupings.

Supplement lighting

Balanced lighting isn't necessarily brilliant lighting. Sometimes, supplementary lights can be placed inside a china cabinet or hidden in its top. Torcheres for indirect or reflected light come in both floor and table styles. But whatever sources you choose, try to have an equal balance of light throughout the room.

If you do use supplementary fluorescent lighting, remember that the tubes come in more than one shade. It's important to select the lamp color first, then choose your wall covering, drapery, and the rug under the same shade of lighting.

Light for play and work

For easier seeing at cards, sewing, and reading, you need at least a 150-watt bulb. But you will need other lights in the room, for your eyes glance about. The stronger one light is, the greater is the danger of too much contrast.

The chandelier pictured is a pulley type that draws down so that beams fall on the cards but never directly on the eyes. Another good lamp for card playing is the swing-arm bridge type, used with a glass reflecting bowl.

Spotlight for drama

Dramatize your decorating with bright accents of light. This one sets directly into the ceiling, but there are exposed models—bullet-shaped—which can be painted to match the ceiling.

Consider using pin-up spots, or photographers' clamps with a spotlight bulb. For example, at a dinner party, hide a pin-point spot and focus it on the centerpiece while the rest of the table glows by candlelight. Or use a clamp light shining on an accessory.

Try luminous panels

Panels give practical illumination, are decorative, too. Here, a window becomes a shadow box with fluorescent tubes shining through light-diffusing ground glass on plastic. Fluorescents are cool, produce a lot of illumination for a very little current.

Try panels like these in those hard-to-curtain strip windows in new homes, or the tiny, almost useless windows beside the fireplace in an old home. This is a striking way to show off any collection: china, miniature cars.

Balanced light flatters decor

You've spent considerable time—and money—in making your home a pleasant and attractive place to live. Make the most of it with the kind of lighting that shows it off to best advantage—and, of course, the kind of lighting that is good for your eyes. The style of your lamps and fixtures will depend on the style of your over-all decorating plan.

Lamps balance general light

Lamps, which provide specific light in a room, distribute and balance the room's lighting. Combined with the wall and ceiling fixtures which provide general light, they assure lighting harmony in most rooms.

Every lamp for specific jobs such as reading, sewing, or working also contributes 40 to 50 square feet of the general illumination or low-level lighting, serving two purposes.

Shades need white inner linings to prevent excessive light absorption and color distortion. Open tops contribute soft indirect lighting and cut down on "hot spots" and shadows.

Be sure that the lamps you buy will carry at least a 50-100-150 watt bulb. This will give you three levels of illumination, for soft general lighting, for conversation, for reading or sewing, or work tasks.

Fixtures are important

In addition to a balance of lamps for specific high-level lighting, you will need over-all general lighting. Plan carefully so that you have an adequate number of ceiling and wall fixtures in your home.

Check your circuits

Voltage will decrease when your circuits are too small, or overloaded. Your lighting effectiveness can be reduced by as much as a third—and there is always the danger of overworking and eventually burning out the motors of your appliances.

Most average-size homes need a minimum of three circuits for general purposes, two for kitchen, laundry, and dining areas, and an individual circuit for each of the major appliances, such as washers.

Ceiling and fireplace lighting dramatize decorating →

This handsome contemporary room is remodeled in a high-ceilinged Victorian home. The ceiling was dropped, and the curve lined with metal mesh and plastered. Fixture holds 300-watt bulbs. The round coffee table was designed to repeat the curves of the ceiling lighting. Table lamps provide local lighting.

Planned light dramatizes any room

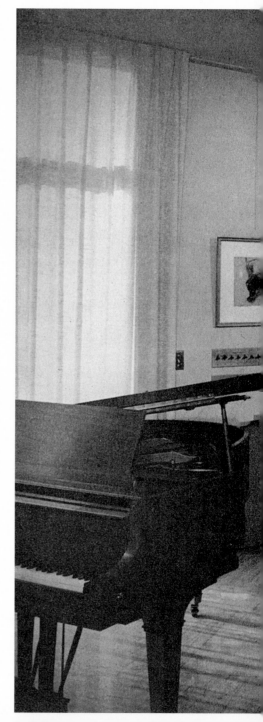

A single pole lamp serves

four lighting purposes

The four lights can be turned on singly or all at once. Top cone reflects against ceiling for general light; second displays pictures; third is for reading; fourth washes wall, creates visual space.

A row of recessed fixtures →

spots a picture arrangement

Set above, but far enough out to bathe the whole picture wall with light, these recessed fixtures also serve as general illumination for this end of the room. Planning is good, because at night, artificial light will come from the same direction as does natural daylight.

Planning for good lighting includes arranging for direct reading light next to comfortable chairs, and for general illumination. But do consider the added value of light as a dramatic decorative feature, too.

Here's where an over-all room plan is invaluable. Before buying lamps or lighting fixtures, decide and indicate where pictures will be hung, where an interesting accessory needs spotlighting. If you're building, it's even more important, for you can incorporate built-in lighting that won't take up valuable wall space, will also do a better lighting job.

Prescriptions for good lighting

Scientific research has proved that following a few simple prescriptions for the placement of lamps and fixtures will give you better light, protect your eyes from strain.

As with furniture arrangement, the "rule" for placing lamps is comfort. The effort of figuring out a few simple measurements before you buy your lamps or place them will pay off in years of relaxation.

Good looks go along with comfort, too. Place your lamps where they will be the most serviceable, and you will find the resulting decorative effect quite pleasing.

To follow these prescriptions for good lighting, first check your furniture arrangement plan. From this plan, decide how many lamps you must have for proper balance, to serve every need. Then check the heights of tables where lamps are to be placed. From our illustrations, choose the kind of a lamp you are going to buy—table, floor lamp, wall bracket. Then, figure the measurements for your new lamps.

Don't forget outdoor light

When you've planned your lighting *inside* your home, consider the *outside*. A lighted number is a friendly welcome, and so are courtesy lights beside the entrance.

If you use a swing-arm or regular floor lamp

The height to the lower edge of the shade should be between 47 and 49 inches. Measure 15 inches to one side from the center of your reading material, and 26 inches straight back to the rear. Place the lamp so the center of the shade is above this point.

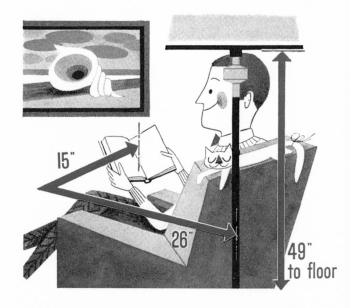

15"

26"

49"
to floor

If you use a table lamp

Table plus lamp base should total 39 to 42 inches. Measure 20 inches to one side from the center of your reading material. From here, measure 16 inches toward rear of chair. Place the lamp so the center of the shade is just above this point, with base in a direct line with shoulder. Shade should be at least 20 inches deep, 8½ inches at the top, 20 at base.

If you use a wall lamp

Hang the lamp so that the lower edge of the shade is 48 inches above the floor. Measure 26 inches out from the center of the lamp shade—usually about 7 inches from the wall—then 15 inches to one side at right angle. Now, place your chair by lamp so that the center of your reading material is at this exact point.

If you need sewing light

For a right-handed person, measure 15 inches to the left from the center of your sewing. From this point, measure at a right angle toward the rear of the chair—12 inches for floor lamps, 6 inches for table lamps. Place the lamp so center of shade is above this point. If the material is a dark color, add a spot or a flood lamp.

If you need desk light

If you are right-handed, measure 15 inches to the left of your work center, and 12 inches back at right angles toward the rear of the desk. Center the lamp here. Distance from the desk top to bottom edge of shade should measure 15 inches. Light-colored wall is best. Use a big light blotter on desk to avoid distracting contrast.

If you use wall lights

Measure 15 inches to each side of center of the desk. Place lamps so that the center of shade is 17 inches back from front edge of the desk. If the desk is more than 2 feet deep, select lamps with extension arms long enough to maintain the 17-inch depth. The bottom of the lamp shade should be 15 inches above the desk top.

If you read in bed

Measure 20 inches from the center of your book out to side table. Then measure 16 inches at a right angle back toward the wall. Place lamp so that center of shade is just above this point. Height of table plus height of lamp base should locate lower edge of shade approximately 20 inches above top of the mattress.

Good light for make-up

An average dressing table 30 inches high requires a pair of lamps 15 inches to the shade center; a 36-inch dresser should have 22 inches. Place lamps 18 inches at each side of mirror center, 6 inches from the wall. Use white translucent shades so there will be no distortion of color while you're putting on your make-up.

Good light for shaving

Use three fixtures—two wall brackets flanking the mirror, one ceiling fixture. Center brackets 60 inches above the floor, 30 inches apart, so there is plenty of no-glare light for under-chin shaving. Center the ceiling fixture above edge of washbowl, from 12 to 18 inches out from the mirror wall, to reflect light down.

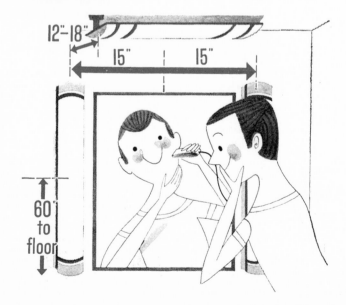

The right kind of light helps your color scheme win the battle against gloom and glare and washed-out or garish tones. If your scheme's sparkle goes down with the sun, poor lighting may be the cause.

Incandescent lights

Regular incandescent lighting will tend to yellow most colors, except a deep blue, which will appear a little grayed, or a deep yellow, which takes on a reddish tone. Colored bulbs in pink, blue, gold, and green provide an easy way to change both the mood and appearance of a room.

In colored bulbs used for reading, sewing, use next higher size than recommended wattage.

Fluorescent lights

Warm fluorescent tubes are especially effective in traditional interiors. They blend nicely with both candlelight and light from incandescent bulbs. Woods, especially mahogany, maple, and walnut, also fabrics and wallpapers, are enhanced.

Cool fluorescent tubes flatter interiors predominantly schemed in cool colors—blues and greens, or create a cool atmosphere.

Wake up your home with the right kind of light

after

← Light-colored, semitransparent shades release light all over the room. New lamps are taller, because height was needed to shed enough light along the long sofa. Valance matches picture mats, conceals a glowing fluorescent light tube.

before

The lighting here isn't doing justice to the room's lovely color harmony. Colors darken and look muddy—little areas of glare compete with vast spaces of dullness. The too-small lamps mean ↓ eyestrain when the family reads or works.

"ISLANDS" OF LIGHT

DRAPERIES LOSE
DAYTIME GLAMOUR

PICTURES
IN
DARKNESS

USELESS
WALL
BRACKET

LIGHT-
STEALING
SHADES
BASES
TOO LOW

TOO
SMALL
DESK
LAMP

COLORS LOST IN SHADOW   READING CHAIR WITHOUT LIGHT

Flush ceiling fixture gives general illumination to the working areas of this combination kitchen-eating area. Colonial fixture over table can be raised or lowered to the desired height, adds soft glow to room.

It's essential— well-balanced kitchen lighting

Strip lighting beneath the upper cabinets focuses light on counter work areas while overhead fixtures cast over-all light for top illumination. Use softer, low intensity lighting over eating areas to make food look appetizing, flatter diners.

chapter 8

Make the most of your
windows

Plan your window treatments for ventilation . . .
for a view or privacy . . . for good lighting . . .
for beauty. The next 26 pages show you the
simple way to window beauty in your home

Pages **231** through **256**

Every window has a treatment

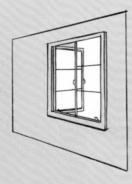

What to do with casements

Blinds hung on each window, painted to match the wall, will give a smooth effect when windows are closed. Or group furniture around the window, tie the group together with a cornice. If your casement windows open in, it is usually more satisfactory to place the fixtures outside the window frame, so that curtains or draperies can be drawn clear when the windows are open

What to do with strip windows

If you want to hide strip windows try blending curtain color with the wall around them. If you use full-length draperies try filling in space below with an important furniture arrangement, framed with draperies

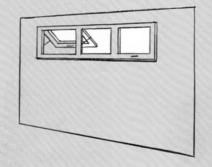

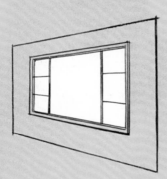

Treating the view window

If you really have a view, make the most of it with a subdued window treatment that calls attention to outdoor beauty instead of to itself. If you need privacy, try filmy curtains for daytime use, plus opaque draperies to shut you in at night

Problem windows

Disguise problem windows with curtains that blend with or match the adjoining wall. Or make them an exciting center of interest by covering them with a color or pattern that contrasts sharply with wall

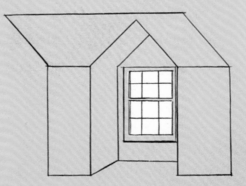

Ventilation, light, view, and beauty

The windows in your home were designed to serve three distinct and separate purposes—provide ventilation, supply adequate natural light, and point up the view, if any. When you decorate, you add one more—beauty.

For proper ventilation, choose a treatment that offers the least possible obstruction to air currents. If the room is dark, get curtains that will let the sunshine in—and supplement the natural with artificial light. If there's a view, choose draperies to enhance it.

Ideas for picture windows

The perfect picture window looks out on a lovely view. It is a little shaded, so that there is never a glare, and it is always completely private from neighbors and from traffic.

Most of us, however, must add the qualities of perfection ourselves. If you need light and glare control, or privacy, try venetian blinds. They fit equally well into a traditional or modern home. Wood slat blinds or woven reed curtains diffuse light, can be colored to match or blend with walls or draperies. Window shades now come in decorator colors,

can be drawn to eliminate outside light entirely. Vertical blinds are similar to venetian blinds, but the slats run up and down, form a dramatic pattern for a contemporary home. If there is no view at all, panels of translucent plastic covering the window will let in soft light as a decorative element. Sheer draperies diffuse glare, leave the view. Cafe curtains let you pull in light where you want it and when you want it.

Opaque draperies are decorative and can be pulled over the translucent ones to give nighttime privacy.

If you lack a view

What's a picture window without a view? Not a frame for outdoor beauty — but you *can* turn it into a delightful background for all your furnishings.

Sheer curtains plus traverse draperies give complete privacy day or night. But you still enjoy the sunlight by day.

Have the courage to turn your back on your picture window, and even put the sofa in front of it. Add pull-up chairs and tables for a grouping.

If you need privacy

If your picture window frames a park or lovely lawns in the daytime — but puts you in a goldfish bowl after dark — traverse draperies are your answer. Enjoy your view in the daytime, pull draperies at dusk.

You can move your sofa over to the window to take full advantage of the beautiful daytime view. Give it company with a pull-up chair and benches, and plenty of reading light for after-dark relaxing.

If you love elegance

Traditional furnishings can be just as elegant in a room with a contemporary picture window, whether it is one big sheet of glass, or, as we show it here, composed of small panes.

Hang rich draperies at the windows and tie them back with ornate knobs. The valance tops them. With sunlight streaming in, it's logical to place your desk in front of the window. But turn it at right angles, facing away from the light.

Arrange for both a view and privacy

If you're lucky enough to have a view, or at least part of one, but still want privacy, consider a combination window treatment.

Hide an unsightly street with cafe curtains at the lower half of your windows—see only green trees above. Combine the cafe curtains with draw-draperies for evening privacy, and your problem is solved.

Louvered shutters will control too-bright sunshine. Hang them either above or below, depending on which part of the room you wish to shade. Or, make your cafes in freely hung panels, so they can be adjusted to cover all or any portion of window.

When closed, shutters will give you privacy—so will the cafes if they're made of a heavy fabric and lined. Then you can just push them back for the daytime view.

Shutters combine with cafes to control privacy and view

Two tiers of lined cafe curtains can be adjusted to show a pretty lawn, drawn together to ward off the sun or insure evening privacy. Double control of light comes with louvered shutters in the upper portion of the window, which can be swung open to let light through, or completely closed.

Strip windows need special handling

From the cottage to the mansion, from the Victorian family home to the contemporary ranch house, you find a common window problem—what to do with strip windows.

One method is to play up the windows, make an asset out of them, turn them into an interesting feature.

In an older home, frame the fireplace windows in a deep shadow box, designed to look like a picture frame. Place a big decorative object in each, such as a bright bowl with tall plants.

In contemporary homes, where diffused light is desired, and the view means nothing, fill the panes with the translucent material that's so often used for lamp shades—with leaves or butterflies in bright colors pressed between leaves of plastic. Furniture placed beneath these windows should have tall accessories reaching up, drawing the eye to the window treatment.

The other method is to play the windows down—to give the illusion that they don't exist. Your material choice may be sheer or opaque, or you might use louvered shutters.

In any event, the color should match walls exactly, blending the windows into the whole wall. The simpler the treatment, the more the windows will "disappear." Furniture placed beneath these windows should be solid, pulling the eye down and away from the wall, with low accessories to catch attention.

A SUBTLE DRAPERY FABRIC

CARRIES ALL OF THE ROOM'S COLORS, BECOMES A DECORATIVE FEATURE

Traverse draperies create an elegantly traditional theme

This bay becomes a dramatic point of emphasis decorated with a wonderful sweep of patterned fabric from side to side. The color scheme is picked up from this pattern, with its color elements distributed throughout the room. The gate-leg table and small chairs are invitingly grouped for two. Underdraperies of sheer casement cloth, or formal cafes, would give you daytime light and welcome breeze control.

Suggestions for treating a bay window

Traditional or contemporary, old or new, America's homes abound in bay windows. They give an illusion of spaciousness, furnish light to many otherwise dull interiors.

The ideal treatment, is to arrange a low seating group in the bay, facing into the room.

Backing this seating group should be your choice of window treatment. If you don't have a view, or want nighttime privacy, traverse draperies around the whole bay would be an excellent choice. If you want sun control, a diffusion of light, and daytime privacy, these draperies could be translucent casement cloth.

Cafe curtains flatter a bay

Cafe curtains make a charming treatment for a Colonial bay. Crisp crisscrossed curtains of cotton or no-iron synthetics would be handsome and suitable. A glass-fibered fabric would be another good choice.

Windows and doors are treated as one unit

If your front door is flanked by either small or full-length windows, treat the whole section as one unit. Shoulder-high cafe curtains here make the hall private, let insiders look out. Ruffled valance gives windows and door one continuous line.

What to do with entry doors and casements

The first requirement for your doors and windows is that they must open easily. You can't just run a beautiful wall of traverse draperies across either, and forget about them.

If your door stands alone, without flanking windows, the simpler the effect the better—usually you would just paint it to match the surrounding walls. If there are windows, treat doors and windows as a unit, with curtains of equal length on each.

If casements open inward, select a treatment that will make them part of a furniture arrangement plan, as the bookcases at the left. Or curtain in a sheer to match the walls, and let them blend into the background.

Casement windows are framed as part of a whole wall unit

If your casements open in, your first problem is to select a treatment that will let you open the windows when you want fresh air. One solution is to frame the window in your upholstery fabric, make it part of a wall-wide bookcase installation.

*Bright color accents
hard-to-decorate windows*

Bright shades draw attention to this window grouping, make them the room's center of interest. Several fabric lengths are sewed together, stapled to shade rollers. Tip: don't hem the sides; use a zigzag or overcast stitch to finish the edges.

Treat problem windows simply

Almost every home has at least one "problem" window—one that just does not seem to fit into any known architectural category or accepted decorating approach. The solution to the problem lies in making a frank appraisal of the situation, then in working out a suitable treatment.

Do you really need the light from the window? If not, curtain it very simply in a fabric that blends with the wall color—or in a print to match the wallpaper. If the window *is* useful, feature it—pick up a color or a pattern from elsewhere in the room, and repeat it in shades, cafe curtains, or draperies.

Blending color, pattern play down windows

These windows are needed for light and ventilation. One is a few inches taller than the other . . . ruffles set at the same height bring them into balance. Sheer curtains blend with the background color of the wallpaper, finish the treatment.

Windows in contemporary homes

Contemporary architecture often features wonderful walls of windows, sometimes following a pitched or sloping roof line. These usually need to be curtained or draped to cut the sun's glare and give a measure of privacy. But the turns or curves at the ceiling line occasionally present a decorating problem.

There are many ideas in drapery hardware which will be a big help, for instance, traverse rods installed

on the ceiling, or "eyelet" rods that will follow any contour.

Treat windows simply

Such "ranch-style" windows are designed to be dramatic spots of emphasis in themselves, and should be treated with extreme simplicity. The fabrics chosen to curtain them should harmonize with the interior color theme and the outdoor view, yet be subtle in both color and pattern.

These contemporary view windows are often combinations of fixed glass areas, plus panes that will open for ventilation. If the ventilating units open at the sides or at the bottom, then floor-to-ceiling traverse draperies are usually indicated. If they open at the top, that portion is usually left clear, since privacy is no problem. A sloping line is best left clear for interest at the ceiling level.

Floor-to-ceiling view window follows the line of the pitched roof. Since the upper part of the window is shielded from glare by the overhang, the drapery line can follow the natural break. Draperies pull back to the wall to emphasize room's horizontal lines, open all of the window to view.

←

Light and breeze control is achieved in this room with tiers of traverse draperies across a long window wall. The pretty print unifies the living and dining areas, inspires color scheme. Glass area along the sloping roof line is shaded by the trees outdoors, gives soft illumination all day long.

What to do with ancient windows

Even if your windows aren't flexible, today's drapery fashions are. Select the right drapery treatment, and those old-fashioned windows will become an asset in any home.

If the window has an unusual or pleasing shape, emphasize it with a dramatic treatment that will make it

Two sets of draperies help widen a window

A wood cornice gives a narrow window new width, is painted to match the walls. Stationary draperies are hung to the floor at each side of the window.

Draperies draw across the window on traverse rods, are cut off short, to clear the radiator. Radiator is boxed with plywood and gold grilles.

Fabric to match walls helps camouflage

Try a drapery cover-up for dated colored panes. If the wall is painted, choose material to match, and paint the radiator the same color.

If the wall is papered, select a material which blends with the background, or a printed fabric to match wallpaper. This creates a uniform look.

stand out, be a focal point in room. Contrasting color in the draperies will do it, or a bold print that sets the room's color scheme.

If the window is awkwardly located, or if it has a bulging radiator under it, decorate the window so it blends in with the room's background.

You may have two windows that are different sizes on the same wall. If so, curtain them to match the background—either in a plain color to match the paint, or a fabric pattern to match the wallpaper. Or cover the whole wall with a sweep of traverse draperies over both windows.

Plan for good looks from outside, too

If you have handsome windows, take advantage of their decorative beauty both inside and out. Windows on the same side of the house should be treated so that the outside effect matches, even though they are in different rooms. Gracefully curved opening requires a special treatment.

A curved valance follows window line

Elegant design of window made it a natural choice for a decorative treatment.

A large formal pattern sets it apart from the rest of the room. The valance squares off at the top. The lower edge follows curve of window, to emphasize line indoors. Valance doesn't show from outdoors.

Traverse draperies are flexible

Of all the possible treatments for today's room-size windows, the most popular, and the easiest to use, are traverse draperies. Even with a combination of fixed and open panes, they give comfortable control over ventilation, light, and view. And their decorative effect can be dramatic or subdued, a central point of decorating interest, or a background for other furnishings in the room.

Traverse draperies can be made of a modern see-through material, or a heavy, opaque fabric. They can curve around bays, or a corner jog, pull to the sides or toward the middle, hang from the ceiling or draw across a flat track on the wall.

Two sets of draperies, with separate controls, are an excellent solution in a room where you want light control in the daytime, privacy at night. Under-curtains could be sheer, ones on top of a heavy fabric.

Combine sheer, heavy draperies for privacy

Semisheer fabric gives daytime privacy, but lets in the light and the view. Heavier, opaque material draws across at night. Here, the underdraperies match the background of the pattern, make a soft background for brightly colored furnishings. The pattern inspires both the color scheme of tawny orange-beige, white and black, and the Oriental theme.

←

Ceiling track curves draperies around corner

In an oddly shaped room, windows close together on two slanting walls are curtained as one, with a ceiling traverse installation. No horizontal break at the top of the window here, to interfere with the floor-to-ceiling sweep of color. Walls match the fabric background, preserve the color unity.

249

Pert cafes give height and width to a tiny kitchen window. The rods extend beyond the frame on either side, the curtains pull aside so that the entire window can be used. Top and bottom tiers extend beyond frame vertically, to make window look bigger. Fabric trim matches wallpaper.

Cafes are an ideal solution to the window decorating problem in a street-side bedroom. Here, the long bottom tier is closed for privacy, while the upper is open for light and air. A deep, matching ruffle tops both tiers.

Cafes are suitable in a formal room. Just be certain that the material is as elegant as any other in the room. Here, sheer cafes curtain French doors, with overdraperies for night privacy.

250

Cafes—formal or informal

The dictionary says that "cafe" means "restaurant," and cafe curtains derive from the tiers used to cover the glass fronts of restaurants all over the world. The variety of heights at which they can be set, for your own personal requirements of ventilation, light, and view, offers infinite flexibility. Cafes usually hang by tabs or clips from a fixed rod, and are installed in one or more tiers. The material from which they are made can be sheer or heavy, elegant or casual. Colors may be bold or subtle.

Sheers— either ruffly or tailored

There's a whole new family of see-through fabrics available today—organdies that stay crisp and billowy, nets and casement cloths that keep their shape, never sag or droop; newly styled laces that fit into contemporary homes; plains and prints; loosely woven combinations of fine and heavy yarns; matchstick bamboo tied together with yarns, gleam-

Sheer draperies frame a garden view, let the light pour in

From morning until evening, softly gathered sheer draperies enhance a lovely garden view, admit all possible light. After dark, white shades provide privacy, light background for subtle colors of desk, chair grouping.

ing metallic threads and even ribbons.

They all have one thing in common—by day they give adequate privacy to the interior of a room, but also admit light; by night they fill the windows with a background of pattern, texture, or color. Remember, any translucent fabric must be supplemented with shades or with over-draperies for nighttime privacy.

These filmy, see-through fabrics should be used generously, because in small amounts they are insignificant. If they're gathered or ruffled, use enough material to equal two to three times the window width.

Today's sheer fabrics are equally right as tailored panels in a contemporary house, or fluffy, feminine curtains in a traditional one.

A tailored print patterns a whole wall, lets in natural light

Translucent panels pull toward the center, cover a wall flanked by French windows. Expanse of print and lightness of fabric give illusion of more wall space. Rod is covered with tubing—drapery fabric glued on it.

Shades, blinds set a style note

The old-fashioned green window shade is now a thing of the past. No matter what your color scheme—from pink to purple, beige to bittersweet—there are blending shades and blinds. Or, you can tack your fabric choice on shade rollers . . . even spray blinds the color of the walls.

Austrian shades plus rich draperies have an opulent air

Custom-tailored to fit your windows, or made at home with a special shade tape, Austrian shades add an air of elegance to any room. Other choices might be regular pulldown shades in a color to blend with walls, or a rich texture to go with other fabrics.

Pull-up blinds create privacy, - fit right into color theme

Standard-size blinds can be installed in pairs . . . one to pull up from the bottom, insures any degree of privacy— the other, to pull down from the top, adjusts for light, air, and view. In colorful tones, they can be used alone, or teamed with bright draperies.

Use ingenuity
in special places

There's an opportunity to have a little decorating fun in special rooms. Paint a favorite recipe on a shade, and protect it with a plastic spray. Or embroider a motif to match a wallpaper or curtain fabric pattern.

Silhouettes of the whole family, painted on a colorful window shade, dramatize this eating counter. Each member of the family "sits" for his portrait, made first in pencil outline on paper, then traced onto the shade and filled in. Add pleated draperies and a ruffle the color of the silhouettes—paint unfinished stools to blend.

chapter 9

Personalize your home with
accessories

Do you know how to group pictures the easy way?

Would you put a fussy Victorian vase on a

Colonial coffee table? These 30 pages show

you how, when, and where to use accessories

Pages **257** through **286**

When and where to use accessories

Accessories on the walls

Pictures and ornaments on the walls give warmth and personality to a room—make it truly yours. Plan them to be a part of your furniture groupings, not as an end in themselves. A big picture or a group can be focal point in room

Accessories on tables

Don't clutter tables with tiny, useless objects. Keep the lamps tall enough to shed proper lighting. Leave enough surface clear so there will be plenty of room to lay down books, papers, sewing, other work

Accessories on the mantel

Fireplace accessories should be neither too skimpy nor overpowering, but call attention to the wall as a whole. Use pairs for formal balance, or set off a group of small objects with one large accessory

Big picture does it!

Before you drive that nail—think! Get *drama* into your wall arrangements. You might try a single big picture for impact. The subtle tones of the picture above blend with the wall paneling and the wood of the dining group. Its elegance is matched by graceful tea and coffee service, and the delicate lines of the Oriental "tree."

One picture can easily "furnish" wall

When you use just one big picture, you have the opportunity of making a dramatic grouping, tying it in with furniture, lamps, and other accessories in a single decorative unit.

Before you hang the picture, set up the other components of the grouping in their permanent positions. Try them out for a while before you make a final decision on the arrangement. A trial period will save unnecessary work later on.

Oriental theme carries a strong visual impact

An Oriental wall scroll creates strong vertical lines to contrast with the predominantly horizontal lines of the Contemporary furniture in this home, adds pattern to the plainness of the basic decorating scheme.

First, the bench was set in place, and then the scroll was hung off-center. Extra bulk was needed, so an important bowl was added to the grouping, with branches giving more height.

Select a painting in scale with other furnishings

This large picture hangs low enough to form part of grouping which includes table, lamp, and flowers. Size is related to the lamp. The flowers are concentrated in a bulky arrangement.

Color is important here, with all of the tones related to those in the picture. Flowers of white, yellow, and bronze, subtly-colored pillows, all derive from the painting. The white picture frame repeats the lamp color.

Accessories make a real decorating difference

Accessories should be planned just as carefully as the color scheme or furniture arrangement. The room below is attractive and comfortable but looks unfinished. See what a pleasing difference there is in the room at the right, after the accessories have been added.

These accessories were chosen for their functional as well as decorative value. The long line the sofa creates is broken by the picture grouping. The shape of the mantel seems to change because the eye now starts at the top of the picture and follows the candlesticks on down to the lamp on the side table. Both of these accessory groups contribute an important illusion of height to the room.

Room is uninteresting

The functional necessities are present here—place to sit, table to serve chairs and sofa, lamps right height for reading. But personality is missing.

Now, bright necessities of a personalized room are added

From hallway to mantel, from tables to walls, these bright accents have added a sparkle and personality all in keeping with the formal, traditional atmosphere of the room. A collector of fine pictures and prints, this homeowner has used them to draw the conversational groupings into a co-ordinated whole. One group decorates a corner, while another hangs in an even line over the sofa grouping.

Use small pictures in a group to create a dramatic effect

Accessories are grouped with related pictures

See what a dramatic effect you can create by bringing accessories together with pictures into one big unit. This grouping reflects the hobbies of the owners. A collection of Early American samplers and daguerreotypes is interspersed with other pieces of Americana.

For distinctive color and pattern on your walls, group pictures together. Some pictures, in themselves either too small or too unimportant in subject matter to hang alone, become as effective as a single large picture when grouped together. Several pictures with a single theme make a good wall grouping. Framed alike, they will make an artful showing.

Narrow frames with wide white mats are usually good with flower prints. Or you can have a mat which picks up an accent color in your room, perhaps one that also reflects one of the picture tones.

Place pictures evenly

Pictures for grouping need not all be the same size, nor need they neces-sarily be framed alike. The important thing is to place them so that the outside edges of the grouping are approximately even. So placed, they look like one unit instead of several individual items. Be sure the grouping as a unit is in proper scale and balance to the other furnishings.

Use other accessories, too

There are many times when the addition of other accessory items, mixed with framed pictures, makes a particularly handsome grouping. If your hobby is collecting Victorian hand-painted plates, add two or three of them to a grouping of steel engravings on your walls. Lead soldiers would be effective with a grouping of pictures of military uniforms.

Here is an easy way to group pictures

Cut pieces of paper in the same sizes as your pictures. "Hang" with masking tape if your wall is painted, or with pins if it is papered. Move the pieces of paper around on the wall until you get the effect you want. Mark the corners lightly with pencil. Hang pictures to fit the marked pattern.

Picture groupings provide a decorative focal point

The effect of a dramatically used picture is achieved in this family room by the use of three important framed prints within still another frame.

The "mat" is the mantel face, painted the same green as the ceiling, carrying through the solid color of the sofa.

The six prints below, related in color and in wood tones of the frames, draw the eye down to hearth opening.

A light, contemporary home calls for modern accessories. Here a school of fish swims across the fireplace paneling. The larger, solid group is placed directly over the fireplace opening to add weight, call attention to the center of interest. The smaller group of fish balances the whole arrangement.

Plan for the fireplace wall

Your fireplace will usually be the center of decorating interest in your room, so its accessories and accents should be carefully chosen.

We all enjoy pictures and prints, but a picture on *every* wall can be as monotonous as none and defeat the purpose of accessorizing, so avoid overloading. Determine the basic decorating theme of your room, both as to color and style. Then put together a fireplace grouping that will be consistent with the decor.

Balance the groupings

There are two kinds of balance—formal, or symmetrical, and informal or asymmetrical. A formal fireplace arrangement could include a mirror exactly in the center of the wall, and flanked by a pair of lusters at either end of the mantel itself.

An informal arrangement of the same articles would put the mirror at one side of the center line, balanced by the pair of lusters at the other end of the mantel. Formal or informal, the method is your choice, and the results should express your own tastes.

Try balancing the groupings so that they relate to the whole wall, not just to the fireplace opening. The fireplaces shown on these pages have been treated in this manner and reflect imagination and good taste.

An informal arrangement complements this cozy scheme

The gleam of heirloom china warms this gracious room. The mantel grouping of the bowl and candlesticks is arranged to give height as well as to repeat the room's accent colors. Complete in itself, this arrangement balances with painting at the right. Both the painting and the mantel accessories are at approximately the same eye level.

Highlight those prized possessions

By grouping seashells under a crystal platter, you'll call attention to their subtle form, color.

Spacing collector's items is important. Each piece in this cabinet stands out, can be easily identified. Don't yield to the temptation of crowding your accessories.

*Be proud of Father's
trophies and collections*

If your husband or sons have trophies and medals and typically masculine collections such as guns— plan a spot for them when decorating. Let the boys know how proud you are of their keepsakes.

Your hobby can inspire color, pattern

Borrow colors from the china

Your treasured possessions and present hobbies deserve a place in your decorating. They are the notes that can make your home different, distinctive, express your personality.

If your collection is important and complete enough, go farther than just display. Use it as the basis of a decorating scheme. Perhaps you collect antique china similar to the collection illustrated. It's easy to adapt color and pattern.

Follow color principles

Follow the basic principles of developing a color scheme that we have discussed before—beginning with the background. Decide which of collection's colors to use for walls, floor, and ceiling, then major upholstered pieces, in this case, the chair seats.

With these, consider the importance of the wood tones—here a beautiful mahogany that fits the traditional style. Next, choose your accent notes, sharper and sparkling, which are the bright blues of glassware and china designs.

Then consider pattern. It is used subtly here, but the relationship between the china and the decorating pattern is still obvious.

Other kinds of collections can serve as a basis for decorating by drawing color and pattern from them.

Basic color theme of blue and white was copied directly from fine china collection. The rug has a motif taken from one of the china patterns—an idea you could copy in a smaller hooked rug. The blue and white seat covers echo the design of the rug's border, repeat swirls.

Decorative plants and flowers bring in friendliness

Ever see a room that seemed cold and distant? A room that lacked a feeling of life and friendliness? The missing element was probably that most taken-for-granted accessory—something green and growing.

The simplest way of using this element is to spot pots of foliage, flowering plants, or vases of cut flowers around the room.

Vines on graceful driftwood
grace Contemporary room

So easy to do—and so effective in any room, is this bold arrangement of vines growing on driftwood.

They take little training, little care. The common clay pot reflects the tawny colors of wall and furniture, needs no furbelows added to it.

Bright flowering plants massed on the copper tray complement both the larger arrangement and the color scheme —are easily moved to a window to get their due of morning sunshine.

Delicate cut flowers
enhance Traditional scheme

A bouquet of flowers from a florist, seasonal blooms from your own garden . . . or a specially arranged composition . . . any of these can soften and enliven your rooms with color.

This bouquet in the French manner repeats the delicate colors of the room, suits the simple lines of the container.

Do consider unusual containers in place of the usual vases—copper mugs for marigolds, silver or glass cups and bowls for Traditional rooms.

Select useful accessories

There are two kinds of accessories. There are those that are purely decorative and hold their usefulness in the satisfaction that beauty always gives, in the necessity of mankind for more than pure function. Then there are the accessories that perform a direct service for you, but contain and reflect beauty as well.

In this latter category include pillows, which are created for comfort, but which should be decorative, too.

There are screens, which can serve as room dividers, or hide an unsightly architectural feature. Clocks are a necessity, but they should be chosen for looks and fitted into the total decorative scheme.

Mirrors, too, serve our vanity, but in themselves can be handsome accessories. A bowl for flowers or fruit or knitting is a useful thing, and so are cigarette boxes and the ubiquitous ash tray. Each can be chosen to also serve as a thing of beauty.

Smaller objects such as trays and boxes can be the items that give the room its individuality. Don't be afraid to show the wide variety of your tastes and hobbies. Fishing flies mounted and framed are colorful.

Curios add character

Many of the decorative pieces we now consider Early American were brought back as foreign curiosities by the men who sailed our clipper ships around the world. A gay little chest from the Pennsylvania Dutch country could hold your sheet music, and live happily with Contemporary pattern and with Chinese figures in a modern setting.

Pillows combine beauty with comfort

To be really comfortable for lounging, the square lines of modern furnishings occasionally call for the softness of good plump pillows. If your color scheme is a subtle one, pick up every accent note in a group of pillows, for the brightness every room should have.

If a room's basic colors are bright, subdue them with pillows in grayed tones, sparked with black or brown.

Distribute your colors so that they accent the over-all color theme without being spotty. Try varying the monotony of square ones with other shapes and sizes.

*Make the most of books
in your decorating plans*

Books are necessities, not just decorative accessories. But they have to be stored somewhere, so consider their friendly warmth as part of the decorating scheme. This pleasing arrangement, interspersed with a few decorative objects, scales the fireplace wall, adds colorful note to room.

Integrate a mirror or clock into scheme

Mirrors and clocks are important, so why not plan to make them points of interest? With the right emphasis, such a common object can look entirely different.

You buy a clock or a mirror because it is utilitarian. Shop for it with an eye to its beauty, too. A lovely contemporary or antique clock can

Grouping centers about clock   This simple wall grouping features an ornate clock, blends with combination of old and new in scheme.

be part of the decorating plan on your mantel, or the focal point above the fireplace. It can be the room's distinguishing or dramatic note.

Mirrors need a view

Always place a mirror where it reflects a pleasing scene. If the room is small, hang an extra-large mirror to further a spacious look.

Give the same thought to its framing that you would to a picture. Actually, you're putting a picture of your room on the wall, reflecting the entire decorating theme. Your choice of frames should depend on the style of the other furnishings.

Mirror dresses up wall   A mirror takes little extra space, adds decorative sparkle to a narrow, otherwise uninteresting, entrance hall.

Accessories should be properly scaled for good looks

Useful accessories contribute to the over-all decorating scheme

wrong

Avoid adding decorative objects that are too small and pieces that are too ornate, or poorly proportioned. Functional objects can be pretty as well as practical.

right

An Early American bread trough holds a grouping of potted plants, massed together for bulk. Bookends are copper warmers.

Keep whatnots off the table, plants and flowers low

wrong

right →

Be selective with table accessories. Place them so there's room to set needed things. On this small table, the removal of a magazine or book makes room for a coffee tray. The flower arrangement is in scale with the small table, low enough to see over.

A large table calls for just a few important objects

wrong

right →

Little ash trays and figures look lost on this coffee table. A few good-size objects, in different shapes and sizes are a better choice. Black porcelain ash tray, pottery cigarette cup, and a painted wooden fruit bowl help to carry out the casual contemporary theme.

Accessories can make a world of difference

Combine Colonial furniture with a documentary print

A few fine old plates and pitchers in pewter, and one or two authentic antique pieces of furniture set the style here. Contemporary reproductions filled in the rest. Color theme came from documentary print, copied from a hand-woven bedspread. Browns of rug reflect hand-rubbed wood tones.

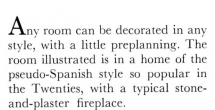

Any room can be decorated in any style, with a little preplanning. The room illustrated is in a home of the pseudo-Spanish style so popular in the Twenties, with a typical stone-and-plaster fireplace.

When the owners decided to build a decorating theme around their prized collection of Colonial antiques, just one architectural change was needed. The fireplace was treat-ed to Colonial paneling. Paint and fabric did the rest. White walls and curtains stem from the documentary print. Blue was picked up for the mantel and for the woodwork.

Heirlooms grace rooms

Even if your tastes are more contemporary, don't pack the heirlooms away. Incorporate the past by blend-

ing antique accessories with contemporary furnishings and colors.

The simplicity of pewter, the ornate patterns of clipper-ship days, go equally well in a room furnished in authentic antiques, or in a starkly contemporary home. However, antiques serve more than just a decorative purpose—they can also be highly useful objects, combining both function and beauty.

A copper wash boiler converts to a container for magazines or a wood basket next to the fireplace. An old dry sink could double as either a television cabinet or chest for holding high-fidelity equipment and records. It could also fill in as a storage spot for sewing supplies.

Old tea caddies make interesting jewel boxes—pewter mugs or bowls are charming flower containers.

The past gives us a heritage of charm

The traditional furniture styles that are so well liked by so many, testify to the wealth of furniture and fabric design left to us by our forebears.

The care and thought which many of them put into their homes reflects a knowledge of fine things. Today, many of their prized possessions are our most cherished antiques.

Fine antiques adapt to today

Many of the pieces which were a part of their decor fit beautifully into today's interiors. A handsome Chippendale chest or a Colonial secretary would become a striking accent piece in a Contemporary setting.

Even if your own preferences are thoroughly modern and your home is furnished accordingly, a study of the ways in which our ancestors distributed color and pattern, and handled furniture styles will be rewarding.

A single strong pattern dominates this room

Strong contrast of black and white, spiked with red, distinguishes this room scheme. The pattern introduces a traditional influence, is massed on two sides of the room, at windows and on the sofa. Accessories and flowers are the only colorful notes.

Modern tables
accent traditional

Against the sharp, clear background of primary red and white, an elegant traditional sofa complements the sleek lines of tables in contemporary design.

Vary styles for a pleasing blend

Don't hesitate to combine the lovely styles of yesterday—18th Century, Provincial, or Colonial—with the sleek lines and lively colors of today's contemporary designs. The only criterion is the final pleasing effect on your interpretation of the way you and your family want to live.

A rule-of-thumb test to follow is whether or not the two styles are of the same degree of formality. If the general effect of your room is informal, then any informal styles will go together, if the proportions, sizes, and colors are harmonious. If your tastes are formal, then combine the more elegant of old and new styles.

Just as a room is more pleasing if one color dominates, so is it more pleasing if one style of furnishings is emphasized. Use one for the bulk of your pieces, accent and accessorize it with contrasting designs.

If most of your furniture is dark, sharpen the over-all effect with a piece or two in light birch or walnut finish, or brighten the room with an accent piece in brilliant paint.

An informal setting combines old, new

A lady's desk in the Colonial tradition combines with a lightly scaled contemporary lounge chair in a setting which expresses the lively and all-embracing tastes of the homeowners. Accessories contrast, adding interest.

Accessories should be
scaled to the space they fill

When selecting a decorative object, keep in mind the size and shape of the space it will fill. There should be a direct relationship between the two. Also consider the object's texture, color, material, to see whether it blends into the over-all scheme.

chapter 10

Space-makers

stretch your living area

Do you need a guest room? Are you frantic for

storage space? Want a separate dining room?

These 20 pages show you the simple way to find

extra space in the rooms you already have

You can find extra living space

Plan your storage wisely

Take advantage of your wall space to find extra storage room. A series of chests fitted together can look like a custom built-in. Add shelves above for books and handsome accessories. Or plan cabinets especially to fit *your* belongings, store your possessions near the place they will be used, make them easy to reach

Get two rooms from one

Use dividers to let your rooms serve more than one purpose. A free-standing chest with shelves above it could serve as a buffet in the dining area, book storage for the living room end. Try to keep the upper part of a divider see-through shelves, so that the room still looks comfortably big

Double-duty furniture

Get extra service from your rooms with furniture that serves more than one purpose. A sofa bed in television room turns it into a guest room, too. An extension table stays small for family use, opens up for parties. A big coffee table serves snacks for family television viewing

Stretch a
little room

Even the tiniest room, like the breezeway above, can be made a comfortable and pleasant place. A triangular table tucks against the wall, out of the traffic pattern. Its glass top gives it a light look. Basket-weave chairs on slim legs add to the feeling of space. The narrow serving table gives plenty of shelf space without bulk. A few bold accessories are used mostly on the walls.

THE SMALL, LIGHTWEIGHT TABLE CAN BE MOVED QUICKLY, EASILY WHEN

SPACE-MAKER 1

First step is a practical arrangement

Consider traffic lanes first, then try to keep as much furniture as possible flat against the wall to avoid traffic tangles.

Chairs at desk and in the dining area are attractive enough to join living-room furniture when company comes. Television on casters can be seen from either room.

←after

↓ before

Too many detours exist in this room's main traffic lanes — sharp turns to avoid chairs in the living room, and around dining table.

AKING UP THE SOFA BED

SPACE-MAKER 2

Color visually enlarges a small room

before

The confusion of color and pattern in this room gives it a chopped-up appearance. A too-small flowered rug, flowered draperies, and patterned chair, all lined up in a row, draw the eye in toward center of room.

after

Large plain areas are a wise choice in a small room.

Here, gray walls and draperies seem to push the walls out. With this gray as a starting point, the floor covering continues the scheme in a closely related gray, black and white, salt-and-pepper tweed which is the only large area of pattern in the room.

Furniture and wood pieces blend with background.

Bold colors advance, pushing strongly *into* a room. Pale colors recede, gently leading the eye *out* of a room.

Here, one of the basic principles of the use of color is applied, and seemingly stretches the walls of this little room. The continuity of color, from soft-gray walls, draperies, and rug, to related tones in the big sofa and blending wood pieces, gives pleas-ant visual illusion of unbroken space.

Even the brighter colors, of green and orange, are grayed, so that they blend with the background.

This closely related color scheme serves as a wonderful background for the furnishings, and gives more freedom in selecting accent colors. Toss pillows, chair seats, and accessories contribute brightening color.

Expand
with light

before

This "picture window" lamp doesn't throw enough light to read by, is not big enough to help illuminate this end of the room. Color and pattern are wrong, the style is out of date.

Placement is also bad. When draperies are opened, both the lamp and table block the view.

after

In the picture of this dining area on page 289, you saw the old, unattractive ceiling-light fixture. This new pull-down lamp is unobtrusive, yet handsome.

For card playing and games, the light pulls down, and, combined with low-level valance lighting, is sufficient. For dining, it pushes up, lights the room.

after Over the large window a valance light reflects up to the white ceiling, down over the draperies. The pull-down lamp can be lowered for close work, or it can be raised to provide general illumination.

Why bother having a corner for a desk or card table, a sewing center or little "den," if you can't see to use it? Light is a space-maker when it makes the dark corners of even the smallest room livable.

Lighting is an important part of decorating. You spend considerable time, thought, and money in making your home a pleasant place to live. Light it up and you'll be delightfully surprised at how dramatic even the smallest room can be.

Dark shadows creeping in the corners give the same contrast as bold colors against pale—and do the same things to your rooms. This darkness advances, comes *into* the room.

Combine lighting effects

Over-all light serves the same purpose as pale colors—attracting the eye outward, making the room seem larger. But flat, over-all light is monotonous, and needs contrast of some color and shadow. Every room should have "something dark, something light, something dull, something bright," so plan for these elements.

after

The sofa bed is the same, but covered to blend with the wall and shrink its size. The large lamp table serves both sofa and chair, is in proper scale to their proportions. The lamp is big enough, too. The large mirror above the sofa reflects the other side of the room, making it seem larger.

The planter-divider at the left was planned so that one section holds books, another stores bed linens.

before

Sometimes the smaller pieces are not the right ones for the smaller rooms. Because this room serves as a guest room, too, the sofa is a sofa bed, and necessarily large. Little tables and lamps just emphasize its bigness. Pictures and accessories are too small for room.

SPACE-MAKER 4

Select in-scale furnishings

In Chapter 4, the discussion of "scale" pointed out it means three things: 1. The ratio of the size of individual parts of a piece to each other. 2. The over-all dimensions of each piece, as compared to the size of other furnishings in the same room. 3. The relationship of each piece to the size of the room where it is used.

The first element is considered in selecting style and design, or the adaptation of the piece to your own height and contours for comfort.

Element 2 is of great importance in choosing lamps and tables. If you must use a large piece of furniture, your inventiveness will perhaps let you come up with a long shelf instead of a massive table, or a lamp that hangs, eliminating need for a table.

You consider the third by making an accurate floor plan, with *all* your furnishings on it, in scale, so you can see where a bulky piece should go.

SPACE-MAKER 5

Use accessories wisely

after

The room now seems larger because a careful arrangement of accessories has done away with the unattractive clutter. Decorative items now draw the eye to important centers of interest. Use only a few important accessories at a time, change them from time to time for variety.

before

This has a familiar look. The pictures are hung haphazardly, with no relation to the furnishings. Years of accumulated knickknacks—and most of them meaningless — are stacked on small, hard-to-dust shelves. Space is almost completely filled, but with accessories that clutter.

Furniture choice stretches space

When space is at a premium, selection of furniture is especially important. Choose pieces that will utilize every inch, even serve more than one purpose. End table, above, doubles as a storage chest—sofa sleeps a guest.

Let rooms serve more
than one purpose

If you need extra space in your home —for guests, for family fun, for working, then study the possibilities of expansion through making your rooms serve more than one purpose.

If you want a television room separate from the living room, perhaps you can find the answer in the dining room, a room seldom used except at mealtime. Try pushing the table against one wall, or get a space-saving extension table that pulls out of a buffet. Then group comfortable furniture around the television set on the other side of the room. Be sure to arrange it so that it doesn't need to be moved when the table is extended.

Put unused rooms to work

Perhaps you have a guest room that is standing idle most of the time. Make it into a "projects" center for all the family. Your desk can go there, the sewing machine and all its equipment and supplies. If most of your ironing goes to the second floor, put the ironing board here, too. You might find that "extra" room in the attic or in the basement.

Rearrangement of furniture created sleeping, study, and play areas here

These boys needed more efficient use of the space in their bed-playroom. Furniture rearrangement provided the answer to their problem.

A table-model television set rests on a record cabinet, pulls out on casters for use. Shelves above hold games and study supplies. Block stools which open at one end so that they can be stacked, provide extra seating and table space.

The low storage chest next to the cabinet doubles as a bench for friends who stop by to watch TV. Mounted post cards make an eye-catching display—an easy way to store a collection.

Twin chests line up at right angles to the wall on one side of the room's entrance in a compact, convenient grouping with twin studio couches. The cabinet opposite houses storage, and the television set. Low bookcases, topped with a row of drawers, make excellent use of the shallow space under the window at left.

Arrangement wastes space

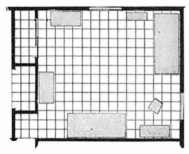

Furniture lined up against wall leaves unused space in center, and limits the room's use.

New plan stretches space

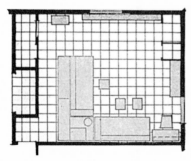

Back-to-back arrangement, and built-ins add convenience and space. The room seems larger.

Lightly scaled desk just fits between bed and opposite wall. Hanging wall shelves add more space for books and collections. A square storage chest fits in angle between beds. Bird-print collection decorates wall behind the bed.

Room-stretching mirrors

If you need light in your room—if you need a feeling of space—if you need sparkle—then plan for an important mirror somewhere.

A mirror seems to double the size of anything in front of it—and a room that is too narrow or too short can look twice as big when a mirrored wall reflects the other three sides. Or a lovely view, caught and framed by a mirror, seems to bring the whole outdoors right into the room.

If your home is dark, multiply the light from the windows by reflecting it into the room with a mirror. Try the same idea with your lighting fixtures and lamps.

Reflect an interesting view

Always locate mirrors where they reflect an interesting picture from various angles—never just a dull wall. The large mirror shown at the right was hung at ceiling level to prevent a distracting line. The mirror adds to the feeling of unity and fills in the space between the windows.

Mirrored wall doubles → apparent size of room

A ceiling-high mirror will visually double the width of a long, narrow room.

Here, it reflects light from the ceiling into an otherwise dark room, repeats the hospitable warmth of the fireplace. Bright note of red sofa is repeated in the flowers and the reflection of the flowers. Side chair adds pattern interest to the scheme.

←

Mirror adds space to a small entrance hall

Make the most of the small space in an entry hall. This narrow, curved shelf is decorative, but does not interfere with traffic. It's convenient, too, to hold every-day purse and gloves. Mirror adds depth to an otherwise tiny space, reflects a larger view. It's handy for quick "repairs" before going out.

give visual impression of space

Make use of your walls for storage

If you need storage space—and most people do—don't overlook the biggest area in your room, the walls. If you are planning a new home, check the possibility of divider walls— where a good portion of the extra-thick space can be devoted to storage.

If you are remodeling or redecorating an older home, draw the floor plan on graph paper. Then see if you can spare 12 to 24 inches of floor space along one wall for built-in storage. In a space 2 feet deep by 3 feet square you can fit a card table and eight folding chairs. Above it might go your television set, and above that, out-of-season items such as the picnic basket and vacuum jug, or the blankets for the guest room.

Dramatize the new wall with panels of vivid color, or with floor-to-ceiling shutter doors.

Built-ins add storage space to a small room

Each of these units is a simple box, made of ¾-inch plywood, dressed up with painted doors and hung with metal shelf brackets. Build them for any room and move them around as your storage needs change and grow. Here, they're filled in with bookshelves.

←

Room for out-of-season and occasional clothing

One answer to the problem of storing clothing is to allot wardrobe space for seasonal wear only. Use hall storage for off-season and seldom-used items. Plan it as a bright decorative spot. This storage wall uses panels of color to break the stretched-out look.

→

A storage wall can also serve as a room divider

This handy storage wall of 2x4s is covered with perforated hardboard, divides one large bedroom into two smaller ones.

There's room for clothing and toy storage, shelves for games and books. A full-size folding door at left provides privacy.

Plan your storage units as part of your decorating scheme

Whether your storage units are a series of chests or ready-made bookcases, or built-in cabinets, plan them as part of the over-all scheme.

Shutters used as doors of built-ins, or panels of burlap or small-patterned wallpaper covering the doors can give texture to the room's decorating scheme. Chests can be painted the accent color of the room, or a dark tone to underscore brighter colors. Or they can be selected in the wood finish of your other furnishings, or in a contrasting finish.

Brighten a bedroom by adding color to the door panels of the built-in storage units. They can be painted or papered to suit your taste. Here, they are covered in gay burlap. Notice how a long, narrow desk fits conveniently, where a wider one might block traffic lane between door, closets.

←

A series of decorated chests adds depth, color, and character to a long wall, gives the solid effect of a built-in, plus the flexibility of change if desired, and counter top for display. Be sure to choose chests that fit tightly together, so there'll be no intervening gap.

Organize a home office

A home office will fit in a minimum amount of kitchen space. Wood-topped peninsula divides the areas, serves as both kitchen work counter and extra desk space. On the office side, it holds household records, files, accounts, stationery, and typewriter. The handy telephone is conveniently spaced to serve both areas.

chapter 11

Decorating ideas for
other rooms

Is your bathroom lighted for shaving? Is there a

place to display the children's treasures? Here are

46 pages of ideas for every room; practical

tips that will add comfort to your home

Plan for comfort all around the house

Plan for hallway convenience

Make your entrance hall comfortable, with little extra touches. A mirror on the inside of the closet door is convenient for adjusting hats. A chair or stool makes it easier to put on rubbers and boots. A tiny chest can hold purses and mail, doubles for storage of odds and ends

Plan bedroom comfort

You spend a third of your life in bed. Decorate your bedroom as a restful background. Choose furnishings that are comfortable. If family members are tall, consider the new king-size mattresses and springs. Plan lighting that covers a reading page, will not disturb other people

Plan convenient storage

Keep your working tools within easy reach—take advantage of new fixtures on the market. A sliding holder for pans works just as well for brooms and mops. Put tape loops on hammers and screwdrivers, hang on ordinary cup holder, or big handy hooks

All around
the house

Whether you're decorating upstairs, downstairs, or all around the house—the living room, the dining room or kitchen, a bedroom, or a family room—the same simple rules apply. Plan for your family's comfort and a pleasing color plan. From the entrance hall to the back door, make your home a friendly place for your family and friends.

before

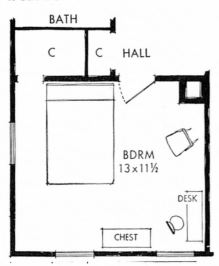

Furniture is badly arranged, and it is difficult to get at things in closet.

after

Now there are two closets, lavatory, dressing area. New lighting is in red.

before →

This 11½x13-foot room was large enough, but a workable furniture arrangement and more storage were badly needed. The placement of the bed on the narrow wall between hall door and closet left no place for bedside tables. Lighting was inadequate for reading or working. The closet was inconvenient, awkwardly placed.

after

The closet wall was moved and the area joined with that of a hall closet to make a dressing room and lavatory. Door to the hall was replaced with a folding door which made good furniture arrangement possible. The built-in unit under the window is flanked by a pair of closets. Room air conditioner and a television set
↓ are painted to blend with the walls.

Capitalize on bedroom space

Most important—is your bedroom right for sleeping—is the bed large enough and the mattress smooth—is there quiet and freedom from light?

Your bedroom can be a second living room, too. Is there a comfortable place for sewing or writing, a place for morning coffee, a telephone, a radio or television set for entertainment?

The bedroom usually serves as a dressing room. Are there good mirrors—with ample natural and artificial light, plenty of closet and drawer space, window treatments that insure privacy?

Is the bedroom easy to clean—with special closet hangers and drawer dividers, simplified bedcoverings, such as contoured sheets?

And is the bedroom a pretty place? You'll enjoy it more if it has a well-planned decorating scheme.

before

The wall where the desk is located was the ideal place for the bed. But this wall had the only wall electrical outlet in the room, which meant the desk had to be near it. Note the floor plan on adequate outlets, page 308 for relation of this corner to whole room.

Preplanning brings results

If you tackle the job of redoing a bedroom in an organized way, you'll save time, money, and disappointments. The first step is to take the list of questions on page 309 and rate your bedroom. If "yes" answers are in the minority, it's time to do something about your bedroom.

Second, list the *good* things about your bedroom. Plan around the furnishings you can keep—and those you must keep. Perhaps your bedroom already has plenty of storage space, but it is badly organized. Or there may be room for a more efficient furniture arrangement.

The third step is the most important. Decide what you want the bedroom to do, and the things you want in the room. You may need a second bathroom, or at the least another lavatory. You may plan to use the bedroom as a sitting room, a retreat for the times when the youngsters take over the living room.

Now, sketch your floor plan of the room as it will be, with all the new furnishings and additions on the plan. Take this plan with you and use it as a shopping guide, so that sizes and shapes will be what you want.

after

Fit furnishings to the space available

It's important to know the dimensions of your room when you shop for furniture. See how perfectly the headboard, night table, and desk fit in the limited wall space. Pieces of almost every size and shape are available for your particular space problem.

Color turns bedroom into restful haven

The procedure for selecting a bedroom color scheme is the same simple one that you follow in decorating any other room in the house. First, take stock of your present furnishings, list those you must keep and work around.

If you are lucky enough to be starting fresh, then the second step is your first one. Select something you like as a starting point, from which to choose your colors. It can be a patterned floor covering, a wallpaper, a pretty fabric, a picture, or a favorite color.

From this beginning, decide on the colors for your background—floor, walls, and ceiling. Next, come the secondary large areas—in the bedroom these will be in your spreads and the covering of a boudoir or slipper chair.

Last, pick out the brighter notes for accents and accessories—lamp bases, ash trays, and so on.

If you stick to the colors represented in the "something you like," and eliminate all others, you can't go wrong in your decorating scheme.

→

Flower-strewn print bedecks this room

All the colors in this bedroom stem from the tapestry-like chintz print. An alternate scheme from the same print could result in rose-red carpeting and spread, pink walls. Or you might choose deep olive-green carpeting, with a lemon-colored spread and slip cover, pale green walls. The trick is to select only two or three colors, eliminate all the others from your scheme, and concentrate on these.

Off-the-floor furnishings

Does a box-like bedroom make you feel cramped and crowded? One way to solve the problem is to use furniture that is lightly scaled and off the floor.

Any furnishings that carry the eye upward will make the room seem higher, lift the ceiling. Furnishings that give you an unblocked view of the floor will also make the room seem bigger, visually push out the walls.

If there is plenty of windowless wall space, furnishings that hang on the wall rather than stand on the floor are good space-savers. Hanging lights instead of lamps will also keep table tops free, give more actual space. If this isn't practical, choose "leggy" furniture to achieve the desired off-the-floor look.

Keep furniture lines simple, and select accessories that accentuate the illusion of height. Window treatments are also important. Keep them light, keep them uncluttered, blend them with the wall color . . . let the draperies run from the ceiling to the floor.

Color, pattern, and style combine to accentuate ceiling height and room size

Classic patterns and colors turn an ordinary room into an exquisite bed-sitting room. Gold and white push out the walls, sunburst pattern draws the eye to the ceiling. A strong motif which includes a Greek key borders the wall, trims both the draw draperies and the tailored bedspreads.

Hanging bedside tables and lights free the floor, dressing stools and lightly scaled desk sweep upward. Even the accessories are chosen to accent a high look, with framed medallions scaling the wall over the desk.

create an illusion of space

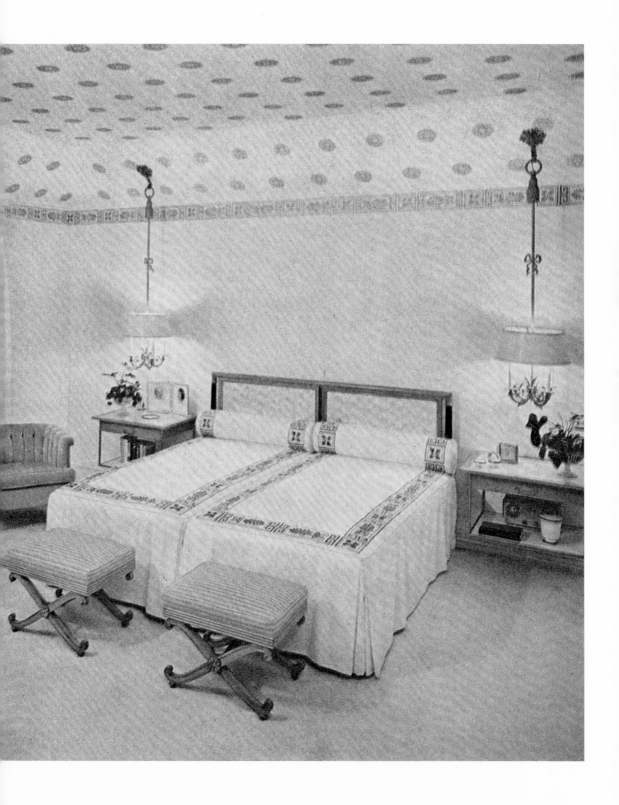

How does your bathroom rate on beauty and convenience?

How many people does your bathroom have to serve—and is it a sterile looking, uncomfortable room? You *can* plan for efficiency and comfort here just as in a larger room.

Consider the luxury of wall-to-wall washable carpeting. It's a tiny investment, and feels wonderful underfoot. Cut it to fit the floor, with holes for pipes, stool, etc., and lay it without fastening down. When dirty, pop it into the washing machine. Saves many a floor scrubbing, too.

If possible, use partitions to separate the various areas in your bathroom. They'll insure privacy, add functional good looks to the decor.

If the whole family must share a bathroom, and if there's enough room, a double sink is a valuable investment, worth extra expense.

Sunny yellow color scheme visually stretches space

Even a small bath can look bigger, if you plan the color scheme carefully. Here, the paint job blends with tile and fixtures, hides the bulk of the sink cabinet. White background of the paper provides contrast, retains the light look. Shiny surfaces reflect illumination from ceiling fixture.

For the bathroom windows

What do you expect of bathroom window treatments? They must give privacy, control light or glare, be easy to care for—and add to the beauty and charm of your over-all decorating scheme.

In addition, curtains should be made of material that is crisp and will stay crisp in the sometimes soggy atmosphere of the average bathroom.

Shutters and venetian blinds can be wiped off with a damp cloth, never need to go to the laundry. Cafe curtains and panels of permanently crisped fabric take to the tub with ease, go flat through the ironer.

Materials that absorb moisture easily are never very satisfactory in a bathroom, since they will soon sag and become listless.

If there is a window over your tub, consider a second shower rod there, and a duplicate shower curtain, to keep the window frame dry.

These pale pink venetian blinds control light and privacy, blend with the wall-covering pattern, and are simple to care for. Colored fixtures and tile inspire the theme, with the bright red accent of the wall-covering design repeated in towels and the bath mat.

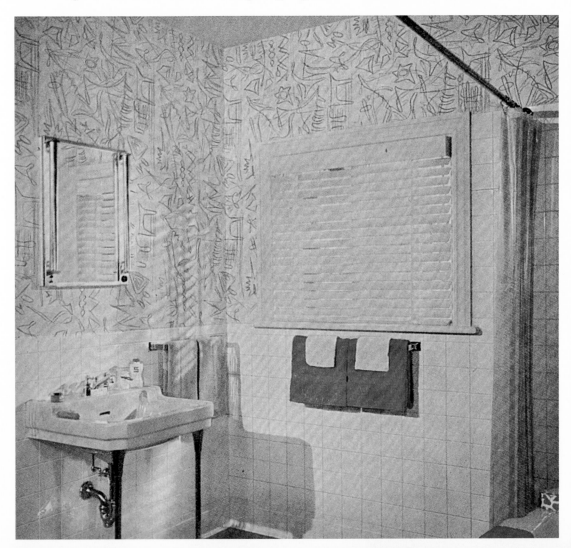

Crisp cafe curtains repeat
white note of bath fixtures

A major color area often ignored when decorating the bathroom is in the fixtures —bowl, stool, and tub. Whether this is white or pastel, the final results will be more pleasing if the color is repeated elsewhere—in the window treatment, wallpaper pattern, towels, or shower curtain.

Cafes in this bathroom are bordered in yellow to repeat the tone of the major color areas of floor and walls.

LIGHTWEIGHT FURNITURE IN FRONT OF THE SOFA BED CAN BE MOVED

Single room leads a double life

WHEN MAKING THE BED

Whether you have guests regularly or rarely, it's nice to know that you can give them the "red carpet treatment" when they come. Comfortable quarters go a long way toward making their stay in your home pleasant.

These ideas will help make a combination den-guest room a success.
1. Since dual-purpose pieces will be used for sitting more than for sleeping, select for sitting comfort every day, enough sleeping comfort for occasional guest use.
2. Leave at least six feet of clearance in front of a sofa bed so it can be made up without moving heavy furniture out of the way every night.
3. Provide space for guest suitcases, such as a folding luggage rack. It can be stored between time, or topped with a tray to become a handy, portable serving table.
4. Leave some free closet space for guests. Or, look for a handsome, free-standing wardrobe that will fit into your decorating scheme.
5. Consider a decorating scheme built around family hobbies—wallpaper with hobby motifs, mementoes, framed maps of travels, pictures that relate to all of the family interests.
6. Light as you would the living room, but be sure there's a good light for a guest to read by when the bed is made up for the night.
7. Make sure there is sufficient storage space for guest linens, towels, pillows, and warm blankets.

Both family, guests share this room

There was a time when the guest room was a sacrosanct spot, kept clean, aired regularly, but never used until company came to stay.

Today's smaller houses, with fewer rooms, make the use of every bit of space important. So the "extra" room usually has to double as family room, television room, perhaps sewing room.

It can serve all these purposes and still be an inviting place for your guests to stay. First in importance is a comfortable bed. This can be any one of the hidden-bed types—a trundle bed, a sofa, or a studio couch.

Arrangement is important

For your own convenience and comfort, plan a furniture arrangement with at least six feet of clearance for a sofa bed when it's opened. Only small, light, easily moved pieces should be placed in front of the sleep-sofas.

Two day beds add up to both sleeping and sitting comfort

Slant-back bolsters come off to reveal full-size mattresses for company. One bed slides part-way under corner table, leaves room less crowded for daytime use. Snack tables are easily moved for access to beds, double as luggage racks. One big lamp serves both couches for reading in bed.

Teens like a room styled just for them

Having a teen-ager around the house is a great joy because of his vast range of interests, his almost day to day, or at least frequent, change of hobbies, his constant fever pitch activity.

More than anything else, he needs a place of his own, where he can work, study—and entertain his own friends, undisturbed by grownups; a place where his friendly clutter can be organized to suit his own taste.

Hobbies need storage space

This is the age where plenty of cabinets are needed . . . put-away storage for all the things he is working on. He'll need shelves, too, to display current accomplishments. And, of course, he'll need a desk for study.

Light is most important to keep young eyes healthy. It can also add to the good looks of the room, serve to spotlight prized possessions.

Bold colors create a masculine atmosphere

Good, strong color, simple lines, give a masculine look to this bed-sitting room. Cabinets are deep enough for almost any storage requirement, help keep room uncluttered. Counter tops provide work space, plus a handy desk. Open shelves are adjustable to any height, hold books, hobby equipment.

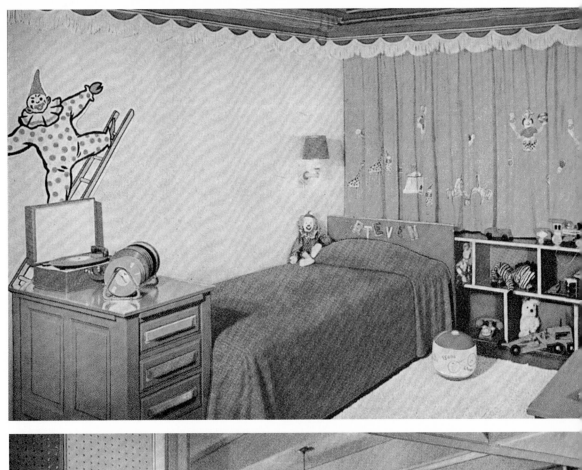

Children's rooms

Color unites odds and ends of furnishings

The top of an old desk was cut in half, painted blue, and nailed to toy shelves for the headboards. Drawer sections of the desk were given new tops, now form storage units at the foot of each bed. A change of colors and draperies will bring the room up-to-date as the children grow.

Color shows youngsters the way to be neat

Bright panels of strong color form a decorative pattern on the drawers and closet fronts of this combination children's room and play room. Lower drawers, for everyday clothing, are easily reached by little ones. Colors indicate contents of drawers, make it easy to find socks, shirts, and pajamas, equally easy to put them away neatly.

Children are proud of their rooms, have definite ideas on the subject. So consider your children's needs and their likes when you decorate for them. Their ideas are often very good.

As soon as a child is out of the nursery stage, the growing-up really begins. Habits and interests change from month to month. The basic requirements for a child's room are good beds, easy-to-care-for furnishings, storage space for toys and books, a desk or table for play or study, and enough room on the floor for games.

Since children love to play host, an extra bed for the special young overnight guest is a thoughtful addition.

Make it easy for them to be neat with deep shelves to hold toys—deep so that there is no danger of the toys falling out, and with plenty of drawer space at a convenient height for the smaller children.

Plan for color changes

A change of color and decoration can keep the room up-to-date as the child grows. The younger set likes bright, primary colors. Paint, wallpaper, and inexpensive washable fabrics can supply this gaiety.

If basic furniture has been chosen wisely, a change to more subtle colors, accessories will bring the room to a teen-ager's dream. Frilly curtains, a dressing table, soft pastels—and presto, it's a young lady's room. Change to simple, rough-textured fabrics, deep tones, and you have a young man's room. An attractive room of his own pleases any child.

Young girls need room for

From the beginning of grammar school on, the house echoes to the giggles of groups of young girls, sharing their secrets, their clothes, experimenting with new lipsticks—and sometimes, even, studying.

Provision for slumber parties

The most popular social events are slumber parties—they stay up most of the night, keep the record player hot, make telephone calls, try on dresses, eat, and gossip.

To keep them happy—and the rest of the family sane—provide a spot of their own where all of these activities can go on undisturbed and without disturbing. Plan sleeping space for their guests right in their own room—it's no fun to be separated. A studio couch or a sofa bed can sleep two extra guests, a folding cot tucks in the closet for others.

Provide plenty of storage space, a desk area with a comfortable study chair, and good study light.

A floral stripe inspires
a feminine decorating theme

A pretty pattern, used with a lavish hand, creates a flowery haven. This room is inexpensive to copy—just as practical as it is pretty.

Sofa bed in the foreground serves two slumber party guests—three in a pinch, lends a sitting room air when only the girls are there. Built-in plastic-topped desks double as hobby counters, a place for make-up experimenting. Bulletin board's a place to display trophies, party invitations, school pennants.

primping, study, and guests

Comfort plus beauty for dining rooms

Both of these qualities are essential in a dining room, and easy to attain if you include the following basics:

1. Storage and serving space—if located near the kitchen, you'll save time putting away dishes and linens, serving food at mealtime.

2. Convenient furniture arrangement—lets you go in and out of the living room and the kitchen without walking around dining room table.

3. Comfortable chairs—provide knee room under table for tallest guest, have well-pitched back support.

4. Good-size table—one big enough to serve expected number of guests . . . if you have a crowd, make it a buffet, rather than a sit-down meal.

5. Good color under artificial light —lighting should enhance the dining room color scheme, provide both soft background illumination and adequate direct lighting for eating.

Colonial furnishings establish a hospitable setting

Dado, woodwork, and the provincial pattern of the wallpaper set off the mellow tones of Colonial furniture.

The chest serves both for storage and for buffets. Hanging light pulls down when needed. The accessories are bulky and important, selected to echo strong outlines of the furniture.

Basic steps apply to your dining room

The three basic steps used in decorating any other room in your home also apply to decorating the dining room. They are:

1. Select colors for major areas . . . floors, walls, ceiling . . . one color should dominate.

2. Select the colors for the large pieces of furniture . . . in this case, the color of the wood on the table top is of vital importance. Next, is the color of the chair seats and backs.

3. Select accents and accessories . . . table linens, china, glassware, centerpieces.

Because the dining room usually adjoins the living room, blend the decorating theme of the two rooms together when you plan. Dining room colors should be restful—limit the bright color to the accent touches. If you used sharp, clear colors in the living room, consider using the same colors—this time in muted tones—in your dining room color scheme.

And here's a tip—if you're displaying fine silver, show it off against a cool color. Warm tones will make silver look tarnished, no matter how often you polish it.

Lighting in the dining room is most important. If you use other serving areas for breakfast and lunch, you'll probably use this room more frequently under artificial light. Provide sparkling, direct light for the dining table, more general illumination to chase shadows, allow for easy service. A pulldown fixture is a good choice for your direct illumination.

White cools rich tones of wood, carpet

Color minimizes the size of the table top. Its soft tone blends with the warm shade of the carpeting. White walls make the room look larger, provide a dramatic background. Draperies carry a tracing of the sharp blue of chair upholstery. Blue, also used in the living room, unites the rooms.

Design details contribute

Add pattern interest to a boxy room —is the result charming, or just cluttered? The final, *successful*, result lies in the way pattern is used.

In a dining room, with bulky pieces of furniture, and a window or two to break up wall space, a bold pattern on the walls or on the floor will cramp the room, make it seem, visually, smaller than it really is.

One way to attain the variety that pattern brings is to use it sparingly, as a trim against plain walls. Let it serve as emphasis of design detail rather than as a feature in itself. It will add height, breadth, and interest.

The soft tones of the walls and carpeting blend together in a subtle, sunny scheme. A generous dash of brilliant white contributes the needed contrast—but the scheme as a whole lacks individuality. Pattern supplies it—in the decorative wallpaper trim defining the wall and ceiling line, in candelabra and mirror frame, in textured drapery trims.

charm to dining rooms

Doubling as architectural detail, a bold border pattern makes this dining roo:
higher and wider. Full-length draperies, which match those on the window wall
undersize and badly placed windows on either side of the buffet. The print is ι
both draperies and valances, makes them an important decorating detail.

Arrangement is the key to use of dining area

In addition to fulfilling the functions of beauty and comfort of the ordinary dining room, a dining area also complements, is a part of, still another area, as a living room, a kitchen, or a family room. Arrangement is the key . . . keep it unobtrusive, out of traffic paths, yet in a place handy to kitchen or serving spots.

Often the dining area can serve another purpose, too. Use the table for a desk, or as a spot for games.

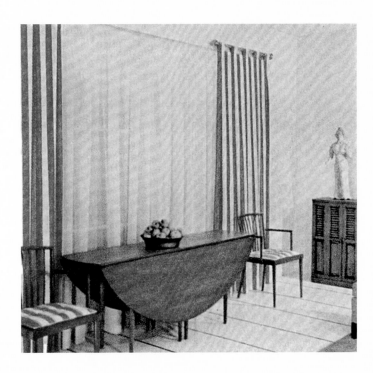

Dining table doubles as a server for buffet parties

This flexible arrangement allows the dining table to be used for many purposes . . . as a server for buffet parties, as a "project" table for family hobbies, for homework or club work.

Plenty of storage for all is in the louvered chest. Colors blend with the general theme of the living room.

Dining chairs pull up to conversation area

Plan for dining area chairs that are comfortable pull-ups for guests. Here, fat cushions do the trick, blend unobtrusively with warm wood tones to fit into the decorating scheme.

Table placed against a window permits a view at breakfast, but is handy to the kitchen for serving.

Yellow sparks a cool blue and green dining room

Pale yellow chrysanthemums crown this table—give it warmth, make it the center of interest. Pale blue china suggests the blue of the walls, the cloth pointing up the green in the draperies. Dominant room hue is blue with a smaller amount of green, yellow accents. Choose white, navy, violet, rose, or yellow for other cloths, mats.

Color scheme your table, too

Just as the wood surface area of your dining table is an important feature of dining-room decorating, so are the tablecloths, mats, china, glassware, silver, and centerpieces. Don't stop your decorating short of these important color scheme ingredients.

Plan your cloths and mats with the

Table setting reflects the contemporary Oriental theme

This table picks up bittersweet from its striking surroundings, combines it with black for drama, white for sparkle, and gold-toned metals for warmth. Candlesticks, candles, chafing dish on black lacquer server repeat the table colors. Celadon green is the dominant room color. Choose bittersweet or celadon for alternate tablecloths and mats.

rest of the room in mind. They could blend with the floor color, or pick up an accent in your drapery material.

China plays an important part. In addition to your basic set of dishes, try collecting services for four or eight that will go with the regular dishes, mix and match with each other to give complete dinner-table variety and special interest.

A set of bamboo-handled flatware would add emphasis to an Oriental dinner. Crimson, pale green, and amber glassware give brilliance to an all-one-color scheme. Candles and flowers on mirror mats reflect warmth.

Elegance is as much at home in the family room as in any other room in your home

Today's dirt-defying and comfortable furnishings let you style the family room to suit your own tastes . . . even elegantly, if you prefer.

Here, a Traditional pattern is lavishly used on ceiling, window, and chair. The fabric is treated to resist dirt and stains, is easily washable, too.

Youngsters prefer bright colors, informal furnishings, places for hobby materials →

The room above is an adult playroom, a second sitting room. If you've active teens in your home, why not turn similar space over to them.

Give them bright panels of color, plenty of pin-up space. Hard-surface flooring will resist spills, and sturdy furniture will weather hard use.

Large or small—you can find a place for special activities

A corner of your kitchen . . . a spot in the basement . . . an unfinished attic room . . . half a bedroom—even a corner of the dining room—any of these can become a gay and pleasant place for family work or play.

Do your young children need a place of their own for play? Then treat a bedroom as you would a playroom elsewhere. Let studio couches serve as beds and place them along a long wall. Use scrubbable, child-proof furnishings, resilient floors. Plan plenty of storage for games.

Do you need a quiet spot to sit down with your husband at the end of the day? Plan a lounge grouping in the dining room or kitchen.

Make it easy for children to care for their things

This playroom could be in an attic, a basement, even be a bedroom. Children can take care of it with a minimum of fuss. Counters are child-height, double as storage cabinets. Colors are strong, make a bright pattern against blue wall.

You can plan a "room with a view" in a tiny corner of the kitchen or dining area

Would you like a Continental terrace? Adapt this to your home by first papering the wall with a mural. Over it tack wooden strips to simulate the window frame. Top it with a prim painted canopy (lights hidden behind will add to the effectiveness). Add a few potted plants, and simple table and chairs.

Color brightens working hours in the kitchen

Work whizzes along when kitchen colors are bright and cheerful. This is one room where you *want* stimulating color.

As in decorating the living room, consider your background colors first, then major pieces of furniture . . . here, the cabinets and counter tops . . . lastly, choose bright accessories.

Plan, too, for kitchen company . . . comfortable chairs for lazy onlookers, counter space and stools for helpers, whether family or guests.

Easy-to-copy color scheme is based on red and yellow tones

Merry and sunny, this color scheme would be easy and inexpensive to adapt in your home. It relies on the buttery yellows of cabinets and curtains, the spark of red-painted chairs for its charm. Accessories echo color plan.

Warm colors welcome guests to a friendly hospitality center

Family and friends like to gather together in this pleasing family room-kitchen combination. Pinkish brick blends with honey-toned woods. For color accent, chairs are painted antique green, cushioned in red.

A snack spot in or near the kitchen saves extra steps

Save yourself miles of walking a year—back and forth between the kitchen and the dining room. The dining room *is* the place for family eating—at the end of the day, for relaxing and for teaching the children the formalities of gracious dining.

But in between, at breakfast, at lunch, for the after-school and before-bedtime snacks, you'll save steps if there's a place to eat in the kitchen. If there isn't room for a table, a pull-down board or counter will do.

A pass-through can be closed off for dining pleasure

There's counter service here for the early morning come-and-get-it crowd—when you're trying to hurry all age groups off to school or office. With the shutters closed, this tiny breakfast room turns into a more formal area, just right for luncheon for the bridge foursome. See-through table top has an airy look, makes small space seem less crowded.

*A pull-up table
takes little room,
adds counter space*

Even a tiny kitchen can make a place for a breakfast or snack table. Fixed or movable, a single table top supported by a rod takes little room.

Curve the corners, to avoid bumps and bruises. A spot like this can also serve for your midmorning coffee break, a desk for planning menus or club activities, extra counter space when baking.

←

Stripes add a varicolored accent in this eating area

Three colors in the same fabric type combine in a cheerful, saw-tooth ensemble that inspires the kitchen color scheme. The tablecloth is orange—chair pads and cafe curtains blue.

Strips of each, combined with black, are sewed together for the valance, used to trim the chairs and to make tabs for the cafe curtains. Any combination of three colors would do.

→

Bright shades stress accessory colors, give a sleek look to a contemporary kitchen

Orange and turquoise combine with a soft, buttery-yellow in a simple window treatment in this uncluttered, contemporary kitchen.

The counter tops are ivory-beige — orange and turquoise appear again in accessories. Shades are washable, plastic-coated to repel dust, grease, and even finger marks.

The window expanse seems even wider because of the strong wall accessories on either side. Big and bulky, the baskets are useful for serving fruits, bread — decorative as well.

Wall calendar keeps colorful track of the days, is attractive enough to serve as a design feature.

New color freshens kitchen windows

Good-looking window treatments are a decorating plus for kitchens. First, decide on the kitchen style—is it Provincial, Colonial, or thoroughly Modern? Then tailor the treatment to suit the decorating plan.

Remember, this is one room where you may have a moisture or cleaning problem, so select fabrics that retain their shape, wash well. Also, be sure the treatment you select allows for plenty of light and ventilation.

What's your family's style preference?

Kitchens don't need to be stark and sterile looking . . . they can blend right into the general style theme of the rest of your home. The most elegant of traditional homes, or the most colorful of contemporary ones . . . these, too, can have kitchens in keeping with basic color, style plan.

Although all of today's major appliances and cabinets are practical, you can scheme them to your home by your choice of color or finish. Most important in establishing a style is choice of backgrounds, accessories. They should be selected with as much care as those in the living room.

Traditional

From the scenic wallpaper pattern to the clock arrangement, this kitchen is a superb example of the blending of contemporary cabinets and appliances into a setting with a traditional air. Pale painted chairs, black drawer pulls, "brick" wallcovering, converted oil lamp and shutter doors with brass pulls . . . all convey the antique feeling.

Contemporary

The play of textures, sleek lines, and strong color mark this as a brightly modern kitchen. Serving counter into the family room-dining area picks up the color of the counter tops in the kitchen proper, wall covering blends with cabinets. Easy-to-copy note: dining table made of wood slats, each colored to pick up an accessory tone.

Blend interior-exterior color schemes

There's nothing so satisfying as comfortable outdoor living, on porch or patio. Make a simple floor plan, just as you do for indoors, and decide on what pieces of furniture you'll need.

Provide for reading light on a porch, for soft illumination for dining outdoors after nightfall.

Plan your exterior colors to blend with those indoors, even though finishes and materials are different.

chapter 12

Take advantage of
dollarsavers

Do you have more ideas than dollars? You can

have good decorating on a budget. These pages

show you how to dramatize everyday materials

into imaginative, beautiful surroundings

Use ingenuity to save dollars

Ready-mades with a custom look

If the budget won't stretch to expensive built-ins, or you're living in temporary quarters, get a custom look by combining commercial pieces into dramatic groupings. Fit two or more chests together, top with shelving. Sectional upholstered pieces can be rearranged frequently

Revive castoff furniture

Remodel ugly old pieces to fit into your decorating scheme. An old-fashioned, ornate work table can be cut down to coffee table height. Remove the spindly legs from an ancient chest, glamorize with paint

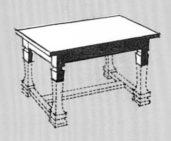

Make dramatic accessories

Make inexpensive accessories interesting by grouping them together in a dramatic way. Maps, excitingly framed, make a wall look important

Do some of the work yourself

You can afford finer materials if you do some of the labor of making and installing. Hang a light fixture—but don't try to do the wiring unless you're an expert and experienced electrician. Paint the kitchen cabinets yourself—but don't try to remodel the sink unless you're a plumber. Do the easy jobs—but leave complicated ones to professionals. You'll save in the long run

Imagination means more than money

Imaginative use of color, skillful handling of accessories, create a delightful room. Check these ideas—

1. An inexpensive quilted fabric disguises bulky lines of old pieces.

2. Commercial dinette chairs sport velvet-upholstered foam cushions.

3. Inexpensive maps, framed importantly, are focal point on wall.

4. Ready-made chests combine with shelving for custom storage wall.

Chemist's materials make fine modern accessories

For television snacks, or candy, try this big 16-inch tidbit jar. Its graceful lines would add beauty to kitchen storage, too. It is just a chemist's powder jar—easily available from a drug supply house, or your own druggist could order it for you. The apples are in an aluminum salad mold. And the nut dish is a chemist's mortar and pestle, made of heavy white porcelain.

Your druggist can provide you with simple, unusual accessories

The big 12-cup capacity carafe is a chemist's heat-treated flask with the neck wrapped in raffia. It rests on a single candle warmer. Centerpiece is a three-way chemical flask, placed on a cork grommet. Cream and sugar are in chemist's porcelain casseroles.

Group perfume bottles for
an important accessory

Why not assemble all your perfume bottles into one attractive and important grouping? This inexpensive shallow basket makes the difference.

A tin cooky sheet, painted the accent color of your bedroom, will do the trick, too. Handsome rose cloche is a chemist's volumetric flask with fresh roses enclosed, placed on a heavy glass cooking dish.

A hanging table saves space, is a point of decorating interest

Less than $10 will add this handsome hanging table to your home. It's a wire frame for drying laundry, sprayed with black lacquer. A black plastic top was cut to fit over the open-wire frame. Vase is a well-proportioned chemical flask.

Eyecatching wall decorations

Inexpensive, but dramatic, wall treatments that change
to suit a mood or show off a new treasure add welcome variety

This hobby is organized into an exciting wall display with perforated hardboard and wire hangers that let you change the arrangement as the hobby grows. Here, a collection of model automobiles combine with simply matted and framed pictures of antique autos.

These sconces cost less than a dollar

They're good reproductions of handsome Eighteenth Century sconces—right out of the dime store. First, they were sprayed black, then the glass bobeches were added. Brass bobeches would pick up gleam of fireplace tools. Sculpture, a low-cost reproduction, continues the theme of the painting.

Children should also have a place to display their treasures

Less than $2.50 provided this wall treatment for a child's room. This includes the shelf for the hobby collection and the hanging world globe. The shelf is a plastic cutlery tray, the globe a large-size plastic balloon hung with green yarn.

These ideas are budget-easy and fun to do

A Provincial air ↑

Mellow, aged-pine look is achieved with antique pine staining wax, traditional hardware added after finishing. Chest is available with base.

An Oriental mood

The table was just junk, but its straight lines were easily converted to the Oriental look. The top is plastic upholstery, with a padding of ¼-inch foam rubber.

Modern in theme →

A jet black stain and brushed-brass knobs, also black iron legs finish this chest. Plastic veneer on top of chest gives a polished marble look.

In your spare time, and with little effort, make this colorful rug

One-of-a-kind rug,
custom-made for your home,
introduces color scheme

It's a dollar-saver, yes, but it's also a unique and personal creation that no one else will have. The rug shown above carries the basic blues and greens of the room's color scheme.

Each strip is crocheted, then joined with the others into the rug. Instead of the greens and blues, it could have carried the major accent colors of yellow, gold, and white, echoing the sofa, landscape, frame, and hanging lamps.

There are many other ways of making such a rug. Sew strips of inexpensive carpeting together, or fashion small throw rugs into one large one.

Create a wall decoration

Put personality on your walls with a little ingenuity— dramatize hobbies, family likes

These oversize fruits are big and beautiful on a breakfast room wall, give a colorful welcome at breakfast time. They're cut from felt—outlines are from a child's coloring book, or from a magazine—and pasted on the wall.

In the living room, you might make a more "formal" picture by cutting the outline of a vase or basket, filling it with stylized flowers in colors to suit your decorating scheme.

For the family room, make little hand puppets, hang them on the wall. Cut out outlines of a tennis racket, a golf club and ball, a camera—anything to represent family hobbies.

Paint a door

Give the outside of your home a lift, too—dramatize the entrance with a colored door

An inexpensive touch, but an exciting one, brightens up your home with a fresh coat of paint on the front door.

For balance, distribute the color somewhere else . . . in flowerpots, in blinds, on a foot scraper, an entry bench, or in the house trim.

The same idea goes indoors, too. Strong, bright color on a bathroom or bedroom door will dress up a hall, add interest to an otherwise dull area.

A simple change transforms your draperies

Sometimes just the addition of new curtains or draperies or the remodeling of old ones will give your rooms that freshly decorated look.

There are three important steps to take. (1) Decide on the style and the effect you want. (2) Remember, window treatments should fulfill four important functions—control of light, control of ventilation, control of view, beauty. (3) See that your selection incorporates all four qualities.

Tie the new window treatments in with your color scheme and your other furnishings. In a dining room, ready-made tiebacks could be bordered in braid to match trim on place mats. Or old curtains could be dyed to blend with a color note in your china and pottery.

In bathroom, gay towels clipped on brass rods serve as cafe curtains, afford an easy change of scheme.

before

Plain draw-draperies cover a small bay window, inspire the room's color scheme. They'll "do," but they add nothing in the way of form or pattern or style to elegance of furnishings.

after →

Broad borders of white, simple tie-backs, transform these straight, plain draperies into a new window treatment. Now they open room to view, are easily set free for privacy after dark.

White was chosen because it is an accent color in the room's scheme. Another good choice would have been a boldly patterned border, repeated on cushions on the sofa, to tie window and other furnishings together.

If the room style had been more informal, draperies could have been cut to cafe length, hung with self-fabric loops. There's enough material for two tiers. Shutters painted to blend with wall color and drapery fabric could be installed in place of the upper tier.

Still another change, using the same material, could be effected by sewing lengths together, looping them in a swag across all the windows, and gathering them through hoops at the corners of the bay. Only simple shades would be needed to complete the idea.

"Refurnish" with paint and
a pretty, printed fabric

New furniture isn't always the answer to redecorating. Perhaps the pieces you now own have good lines, but are just faded and need refinishing . . . or a good coat of paint.

One good way to save dollars in redecorating is to choose a printed fabric you like, use it lavishly in your room. From it, select a color for newly painted walls, another color to serve as an accent for painted furniture . . . a chest, table, or dresser.

← *One big, bold print sets both pattern and color scheme in an elegantly redecorated bedroom*

The pattern of the print dictated its use in this room. Stiffened with quilting, it curves gracefully as a spread. Quilted again, it covers two matching side chairs. Scalloped valance follows the pattern line of the print.

A subtle white was picked up for new color on the walls, combined with black diamond insets for the flooring. The old, elegant headboard and dresser, with its companion mirror, were painted a soft blue with touches of white. Rest of furniture stayed the same.

Ready-made draperies, new paint color, a new dust ruffle, transformed this room

Soft, quiet colors perform two services here. First, they are fresh and appealing. Second, the blending tones reprieve a cut-up room, make it seem bigger. The only changes here were the addition of a dust ruffle to a too-small bedspread, draperies, and a new wall color to tie them together.

Another color scheme could repeat the gold tone of the chair on the wall, in draperies, and ruffle; or use white in walls and draperies, a gold dust ruffle and lamp shade.

Dollar savers also let you splurge

The biggest trouble with a fixed budget is that it's so *fixed*. One of the best ways to help you ignore it is to combine your spendthrift urges together with large helpings of elbow-grease, doses of do-it-yourself, and of making things do.

You know the general effect you want to achieve in your home. Make a list of all the furnishings and accessories you'd like to have. Now check those items which *must* be bought, which *must* be of the best quality and design to get the desired results.

Splurge on those items—don't compromise on quality, because they will set the rich tone of your home. Plan to make as many of the other things as you can . . . curtains, draperies, screens, bookshelves. Find older pieces of furniture with good lines—pieces that you can refinish to blend with more expensive buys.

Consider the popularity and effectiveness of painted pieces for accents . . . a series of unfinished chairs, each colored in one of the accent tones . . . or a small chest which picks up a bright note from patterned upholstery, draperies, or wallpaper.

High quality and comfort in upholstered pieces blend with do-it-yourself refinished tables

The living room sofa not only has to serve as daily seating for an active family, but must double as a guest-bed, too. Here's a place where cutting costs would be an extravagance, because this piece must be sturdy, to take daily use and last for years.

The family still wanted both drama and comfort, so imagination went to work in the rest of the room. An old dining room table, cut down and refinished, serves as a coffee table.

Cleverest touch in the room is the screen which divides the living area from the dining room. Bright canvas panels in the major accent color create a Mondrian-type pattern screen.

Bookshelves "furnish" a wall, add color and pattern at ← comparatively small expense

Floor-to-ceiling shelves loaded with books and magazines contribute to the lived-in look that sets the pattern for this home's hospitality and cheer.

Simple for an amateur carpenter to make, they help give an illusion of height to the room. The amount saved on doing this project themselves will help buy the books and magazine subscriptions this family enjoys.

Another do-it-yourself "plus" is the exciting use of color. Living room walls are neutral to blend with the free-standing fireplace, but ceiling and floor are vibrantly colorful.

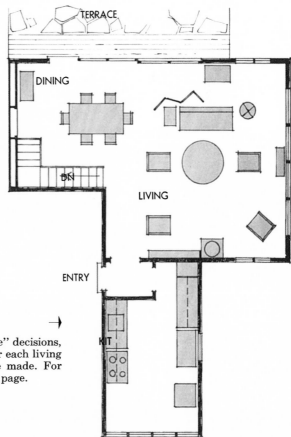

Before this family made its "splurge or save" decisions, a floor plan was drawn, and exact needs for each living area determined. Then, final choices were made. For their exciting color co-ordination, turn the page.

*Co-ordinate colors
and styles
throughout house*

This is the dining end of the living-dining room shown on the preceding page. Here, the walls take on the tone of the vibrant ceiling, create a warm, pleasing background for dining.

Because the color is so intense, no other note is introduced into the scheme. The painting and furniture blend, only accessory note is white.

Basic color choice links every room in the house

*Neutral color
subdues
brilliant orange*

Because appliances in this kitchen are white, this useful neutral takes a greater part in the decorating . . . carrying the color onto walls, into accessories. Yellow . . . related to the orange . . . was chosen as a second bright color. Shutters frame the pass-through to the hallway.

chapter 13

Redecorating
makes your dreams come true

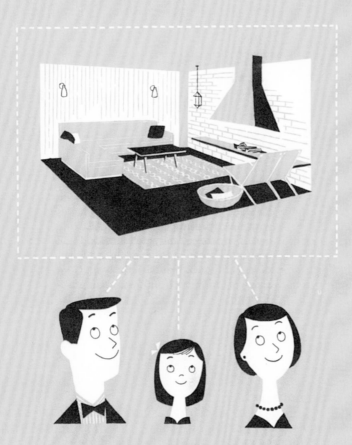

It's easy to decorate when you follow the

simple "how-to" steps in this book. The following

pages show you just how other families like

yours achieved the homes of their dreams

You can do it, too

Change backgrounds

Give your home new lilt and sparkle with a fresh, bright background. Change the colors and the patterns on your walls, and see how excitingly different the furniture will look. Banish the dull and dingy look of an old house with new color

Pep up with new fabrics

Change the shape of those old-fashioned windows with new curtains or draperies. Replace old opaque paper lampshades with new transluscent ones of plastic or one of the sheer "miracle" fabrics. Hide the bulky lines of an old chair with a slipcover that blends with the wall. Give a new sparkle with pillows, chair seats of some dramatically bright material

Combine old and new things

Find an exciting new atmosphere by combining your treasured furnishings with gay contemporary designs. Just remember to mix formal with formal, casual styles with casual, for the best results. Don't try to match finishes— a room looks best with a contrast of dark and light. Perk up traditional mahogany with a modern chest painted a bright accent color. Or emphasize dark tones with blond pieces

Pick a new
color scheme

Even if you're on a strict budget, you can gain new beauty with an inexpensive change in color scheme. On the next page, you'll see the "before" of this bedroom. Ready-made bedspreads, draperies, a coat of paint on an old chest, a wallpaper dado, bright accessories, transform this room.

before

Furnishings are sturdy enough, but dreary

These *are* good mattresses and springs, most comfortable for refreshing sleep. And there's plenty of storage space in the old chest. But, this room represents only half of the requisites for good decorating. Physical comfort is evident, but beauty's lacking.

Accessories add the finishing touch to decorating scheme

after

Accessories, colors create Colonial charm

Just as in the other version of this room on the preceding page, pattern and color achieved charm at little cost. Ready-made bedspreads, a wallpaper dado with draperies of a matching fabric, painted chest . . . these make the vital difference. Coach lamps on the walls add to the style, free chest-top for other items. A collection of keys mounted as a picture, groups of inexpensive prints, green bench, finish the room.

Fresh colors spruce up old furniture

Even if you are on a strict budget—or if your home is a temporary one, or rented, and you dislike investing much in someone else's property—you can still enjoy the delight of lovely surroundings that reflect your family's living preferences.

Plan just as carefully as you would for the most luxurious home. The procedure's the same—and you'll save yourself costly mistakes by planning before buying.

Color makes difference

Even if your style is "Early Attic" or "Contemporary Cellar"—the heterogeneous collection of family castoffs—you can make them all part of a harmonious and pleasing room if you employ an imaginative color plan.

Big, overstuffed, or bulky pieces lose their ugly lines when slip-covered in plain material to match the walls. Two or three diverse chairs look as though they belonged together when covered with matching fabric or related colors.

A single fabric, a simple color scheme, carried throughout the house, will help disguise all these odd furnishings. Your home will reflect your good taste—look well-planned, loved, and welcoming to your guests.

A QUILTED FLORAL PRINT

PULLS TOGETHER A COLLECTION OF FAMILY HAND-ME-DOWNS

A drab wall is a candidate for new look

before

Typical of the situation in many older homes, the furnace chimney caused an awkward break in the living room wall, prevented logical furniture arrangement. Tiny windows on either side were difficult to curtain, almost useless.

after →

Remodeling turned this wall into a dramatic focal point. A translucent panel covers the window area to the right of the chimney, lets in soft light. Window wall area at the left was paneled in prefinished wood, which blends with the new furniture finishes.

Most important step was the installation of a platform set with ceramic tile . . . big enough to serve for plants, as a seat, and as a base for a freestanding fireplace. Contemporary furnishings and vividly colored accessories complement the remodeling.

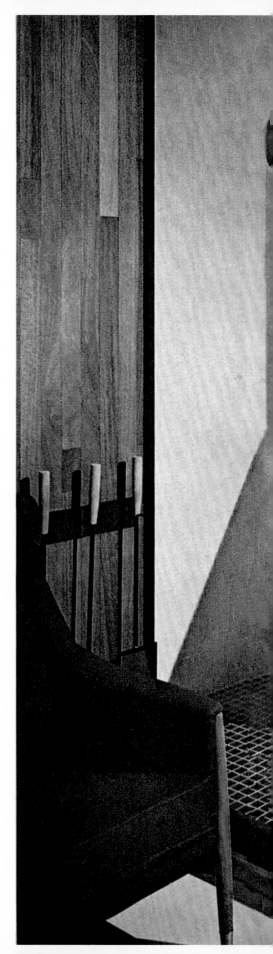

Contrast of red and white added to basic color scheme adds a new vibrancy

Rearrangement of furniture, accessories, plus bright color, two new chests and benches, make the difference. Furniture placement lets traffic flow easily, makes the most of seating. Useless tops came off corner tables, leaving them free for important accessories. Fireplace grillwork and papered panel pick up red. Ceiling spots dramatize the room.

Add sparkling accent hues

Formula for rehabilitating a tired room:
1. Rearrange furniture to get the most out of the available space.
2. Add new pieces where needed.
3. Most important . . . add a few vibrant touches of color to pep up the room. Distribute this new color around the room for pleasing balance.
4. Dramatize the room with light, to enhance the new color changes.
5. Rearrange old accessories, add new ones that are nobly scaled.

before

A massive fireplace wall, good furniture with fine lines, good basic color . . . yet this room is dull and dreary. It looks cluttered, and the floor space is broken up with too many pieces . . . the traffic pattern is difficult to follow.

after

Fabric panels, emphasized with contrasting color, redo the room. Canopy bed adds a distinctive touch. Painted chest contributes cheerful color, repeated in coverlet and draperies. Stairway is perfect spot to show off brass, copper, and growing plants.

Emphasize good details

Lurking in the background in your home may be truly distinguished detail, so hidden by your decorating that you can't see it. Handsome panels, architectural design, can be emphasized to bring out the true beauty of your home.

And if it doesn't exist—invent it. Use decorative moldings to establish panel outlines, chair or plate rails.

before

Handsome paneling looks insignificant, almost hidden under nondescript color. Furniture has nice lines, but does not show to advantage. Bed is undistinguished, adds nothing to decorative possibilities.

after

The only new item is the round table. Credenza moves from windows to wall, freeing traffic path to kitchen. Break-front is more suitable in the living room. Bright paint on the old chairs, striped fabric on seats and Roman shades supply unifying color.

Add color and rearrange for spacious look

Sometimes the accumulation of clutter collected over the years is so familiar, we don't even see it. Take a good look at your home—pretend it isn't yours—and see if some shifting about, some consolidation, and some reorganization might give a room a whole new look.

before

One-two-three—everything centers along a wall, or in the middle of the floor, obstructs the traffic path, fills the room. Color is drab and uninteresting, lacks a dramatic note of interest.

after

Plan a traveling decorating scheme

Even if your family is one of the many that must often uproot and move to a new town, it's possible to take your decorating scheme along.

A series of rugs in the same color, enough matching chests to be dramatic when grouped in a big room—separated for a small one, pair of loveseat-size sofas rather than one big one . . . all will allow a repeat of your decorating theme. Just add chosen color to the new walls.

Groups of storage pieces will fit in any home

Tall and important, the color-paneled wardrobes are designed for hall storage here, can double as extra closets or an entertainment wall in another home. They can also be used separately. Grass-square rug can be resewn to fit space requirements.

chapter 14

Adequate Wiring

is an essential ingredient

Behind every well-planned home there is

sufficient housepower—the basic element which

insures an adequate, safe electrical supply

where and when it is needed

Up-to-date wiring gives good service

Wiring for the workshop

For full enjoyment of your workshop, and to guard against burned-out motors, plan for a special branch circuit that provides current for small-load power tools and for a second, independent circuit to drive heavier tools properly.

Preplanning pays off

If you're building a new home, include plans for the electrical system during the blueprint stage. Locate outlets in relation to future furniture arrangement. List present and future equipment to get a clear idea of wiring needs.

Out-of-doors lighting

When planning rewiring, put in enough circuits to handle outdoor needs. Create an outdoor "floor plan" that shows where outlets are needed. Be sure outlets, wiring are weatherproofed. Consider burying wiring to prevent tripping.

Your decorating plans should include provision for
adequate wiring

While you're planning placement of a television set in the living room, appliances in the kitchen, and reading lamps in the study, remember that adequate wiring is a basic need of all these areas of the home.

Four out of five homes are under-wired, and even two-thirds of today's *new* houses are not properly serviced by electricity. So when you remodel or redecorate, make the wiring as up-to-date as the rest of your home.

How do you know if your wiring is adequate?
Check this list to see if these symptoms describe your home?

▶ Lights dim or flicker when appliances go on.
▶ Appliances are slow starting, slow operating.
▶ Fuses blow or circuit breakers trip too often.
▶ Radio fades or is scratchy when appliances go on.
▶ The television picture shrinks.
▶ Outlets and switches seem scarce when you need them.
▶ Several appliances are on the same connection.
▶ Extension cords are in common usage around the house.
▶ Motors overheat too easily in workshop, kitchen, etc.

If these troubles are found in your home, quit blaming appliances—look for substandard wiring. Inadequate wiring costs you money, creates problems. While you're wasting electricity by loss of current, you're getting only partial use of appliances.

Too many appliances in use at the same time will overload undersize wire. Unless fuses or circuit breakers of the proper size guard against this, wire gets overheated and may cause a fire. Your appliances themselves can be seriously damaged when they're starved for electric current—another important reason for adequate wiring.

This is a well-wired home

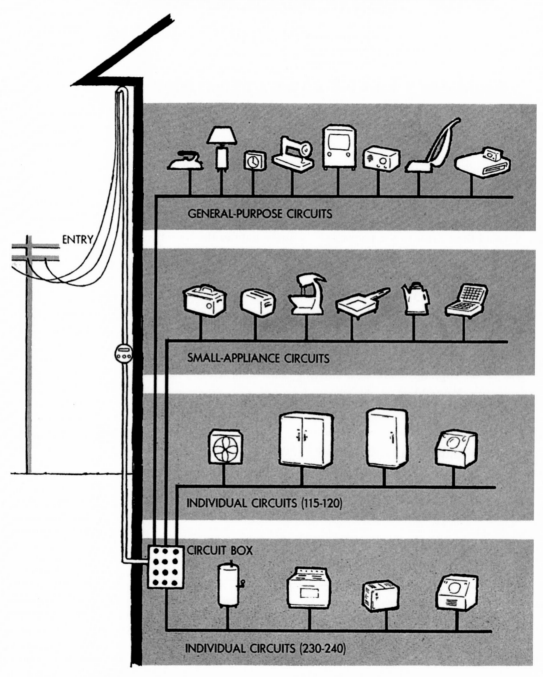

This well-wired home has a three-wire service entrance with a circuit breaker or main switch of at least 100 amperes. Branch circuits include one general-purpose circuit for every 500 square feet of space for lights and convenience outlets. At least two small-appliance circuits are needed for portable appliances. Larger equipment calls for an individual circuit for servicing each of those appliances.

Adequate wiring is essential

Manufacturers have given us more and better electrical equipment to prepare our food, light and heat our homes, and operate the many household motors of a modern dwelling.

But we're not getting top service from these electrical home managers if we fail to do our part—provide proper wiring and circuits.

Most electrical codes specify a 60-ampere, three-wire service entrance into your house. That's minimum. It's not enough power for a home designed for today's living. The Adequate Wiring Bureau recommends a 100-ampere entrance. That's better; but you still may find yourself short of extra current for outdoor lighting, air conditioning, new appliances.

To prepare for today and the future, a 200-ampere service entrance is recommended for your new home. With this reserve power available "at the door," your contractor can give your house a first-class interior and exterior wiring system.

The service entrance should supply 4500 watts for lighting and plug-in appliances, plus additional wattage for major appliances. Minimum 100-amperes supplies 24,000 watts.

Kitchen

Individual circuits of 230 volts should service such appliances as range, oven, and washer-dryer. Dishwasher, disposer, and refrigerator should be on a circuit designed for 115- or 120-volt appliances.

Small-appliance circuits of 115 volts for the coffee maker, toaster, and the like, take loads up to 2300 watts. A 115-volt general-purpose circuit will take care of lighting.

For maximum convenience and efficiency in operating small kitchen appliances, you should have a convenience outlet for every 4 feet of work counter, plus outlets for refrigerator, planning desk, and at table space (for the coffeepot, etc.).

Strip or molding outlets are an easy, effective answer to adding outlets in remodeling. And it's no news today that there are now two, three, and four outlets in a single panel.

Living areas

A circuit plan for the typical living area has a 120-volt general-purpose circuit for fixed and portable lights.

A 120-volt small-appliance circuit services convenience outlets for plug-in appliances, such as radio, television, and portable fans.

Three-wire circuits, rarely found in older homes, supply 4800 watts while the smaller two-wire circuits supply only 2400 watts.

If you're taking real advantage of modern living standards, you'll have provisions for at least one individual 120- or 240-volt circuit coming into your living area, allowing a special cooling or heating unit, such as a room air conditioner.

While this three-circuit living area is more than most homes have (even newly built homes), experts maintain that it is still on the conservative side for electrical use foreseen by 1970. Even more current will be needed.

A sensible start to wiring modernization in older homes is with appliance and convenience circuits. Usually the existing wiring can be used to provide the lighting essential for good vision in the living area.

Workshop, laundry, utilities

An adequately wired workshop must have its own branch circuits—that is, lines that lead from an electrical-distribution box (the main service panel) to lights, appliances, and equipment around the house.

Within the shop, one circuit provides 110/120-volt current for small-load power tools: portable saws, drills, sanders, jigsaw, router, and so on. To drive heavier tools properly—table saw, jointer, belt-disk sander, lathe, multipurpose power tool—the best setup allows a second, independent circuit of 220/230 volts.

Both circuits can be run separately from the main service panel or split off one branch circuit through a distribution box in the shop.

Laundry equipment, too, needs individual circuits for major items.

Water heater and heating plant are generally adequately supplied with power by lines installed by plumbing and heating contractors. The heating plant should be on its own circuit.

In the laundry, though, where you may add extra equipment from time to time, you may need special-purpose circuits. A clothes dryer, for instance, needs delivery of 4500 watts to make it a practical and economical investment. Your washer, too, needs an individual circuit to supply its needed 700 watts. A 110/120-volt line will do that job.

If you've lumped your laundry equipment in one utility room, experts agree you will need a small-appliance circuit with convenience outlets to feed your hand iron, sewing machine, and similar small appliances you may own.

Sleeping area

In general, electrical needs for the bedrooms are about the same as for your living area.

A 120-volt small-appliance circuit will handle such items as radio, television, portable fans, or an electric blanket. In addition, you'll want a 120-volt circuit for fixed and portable lighting fixtures.

You may also want an individual 120- or 240-volt circuit in the sleeping area for a special cooling or heating unit, as an air-conditioner.

Have experts help you with your wiring

When planning the electrical system of a new home or a remodeling project, turn to your local utility company for assistance. They're stocked with informative booklets and staffed with informed personnel. Both can give you good advice—most of it free.

Many local utilities will estimate the cost of new wiring. They may also recommend reliable electrical contractors to bid on the job.

You can pay for your new wiring in two ways. You may be able to finance wiring improvements through your local utility company. Often arrangements are made to pay for the new wiring in a series of monthly premiums added to your service bill. Electrical improvements are also eligible under F.H.A. Title 1 loans.

However you tackle your home-wiring improvements, the new security, efficiency, and actual savings mean a better and safer home.

Make an equipment list before planning new home wiring

By listing all the existing electric appliances and equipment which you now own and plan on acquiring, you'll have a much clearer picture of your present and future wiring needs. Preplanning made this kitchen-laundry possible. Adequate wiring permits the grouping of all the kitchen appliances, the washer and dryer, even the television set, plus good lighting, in one central area.

When you plan your home's wiring, be sure to investigate the many new electrical ideas. They include low-voltage switching, variable light control, silent or glow-in-the-dark switches. The glow-in-the-dark switches are a good idea for use in entrance halls, children's rooms, and bathrooms. Minimum wiring job runs about 2 per cent of new home price—fully adequate wiring costs just another 1 per cent. It's cheap enough insurance for many years of convenient, trouble-free electric living.

How many circuits ... how many outlets are needed?

Just what are your lighting needs? First, figure them out on paper. Make a floor plan of the house. Sketch all existing outlets on this plan and identify the corresponding circuits. Also sketch every lamp, fixture, appliance of any kind in every room, including the basement and attic. To each room, in another color, add items you may buy later, for instance, another television set, an air conditioner, a dishwasher. Your contractor will be able to tell at a glance just where work should be done. Perhaps all you need is rearrangement of existing outlets—perhaps additional circuits.

Plan for balanced lighting, too. Add furniture outlines to the wiring floor plan, and allow for any possible furniture moving—shifting a table when you have company. You'll be able to see at a glance just where new outlets are needed. Be sure the room illumination is well-balanced with provision for both direct and general lighting.

In the living-dining room above, lighting sources are spread throughout the entire room. Lighting is flexible—you can spotlight one area, dim another to suit activities. The two areas become one big room when the chandelier is raised, the table set in a corner. Lamps, coffee table on casters, are easily moved from one spot to another.

Ceiling spots flatter room

If you're building or remodeling, it's a good time to consider installing ceiling spotlights. They can be used as lighting for decorative accents, some seeing tasks, or as general illumination. Balance with upward light from lamps, other fixtures.

Individual spots give direct or general light

These ceiling spotlights distribute functional lighting over the individual furniture groupings, provide additional general illumination. The addition of portable lamps would supplement the light supplied by the ceiling spotlights.

Low voltage switching adds convenience to your home

An outstanding advance in electrical systems is low-voltage switching. You may have heard of it as "remote control," "l-v" (for low-voltage), or "multi-control switching."

Some folks have added a little confusion by calling this system low-voltage "wiring" instead of switching. True, it uses low-voltage "doorbell" wire leading from switches. But all the lights and outlets still feed from the usual 115-volt current.

How does it work?

You can compare low-voltage switching with your automobile's electrical system. When you press a car's starter, you're not working directly with the strong surge of electricity needed to operate the starter motor. A spark of current travels from dashboard to a magnetic relay. This commands battery's full punch to start engine.

In a house, you press a touch-plate switch and a small (24-volt) flash of current notifies a relay (grouped near service entrance, or, in some systems, right at the fixture). A magnetic switch then opens, and the full 115-volt current is sent to do whatever task you have in mind.

Simple as that! But why is this better than the standard method of switching? The one where a wall switch operates as a gate through which the actual current flows?

With low-voltage switching, a dangerous shock at the switching point is no longer possible. This means low-voltage switching is a natural for outdoor use, the laundry, kitchen, workshop, or other areas where shock's more of a potential hazard.

The smaller current load allows much smaller wire than in a conventional system. This wire is easy to drag through a wall; it requires no rigid conduit or other bulky bindings and insulators.

What's the biggest feature?

The thing that makes this system so popular in today's sprawled out, "ranch-style" houses is its remote and multi-control characteristics. To control one light from two points, conventionally, you have to double heavy, expensive 115-volt wire running between switches. To add a third control gets costly and complicated. Remote control over a great distance shoots cost up in a hurry when you're stringing out doubled Number-12 wire, plus conduit.

With low-voltage switching— where one magnetic relay works the light—it's no trick to have a third or fourth control to every one of the lights. And with the cost of low-voltage wire and switches less, there's no reason why you can't enjoy complete mastery of your home's lighting. This means an end to groping into a dark room looking for a switch.

Costs of a low-voltage or a conventional system are about the same in a small house—or in a house over 2,000 square feet (where long halls and large rooms necessitate multi-switching). Costs for low-voltage switching in a medium size house are slightly more than for conventional.

chapter 15

Index

Plan your furniture arrangements the easy way;
sketch the floor plan of your room on the back
of this page—the scale is ¼'' to the foot. Trace
outlines of furniture pieces on pages 391, 393, 395

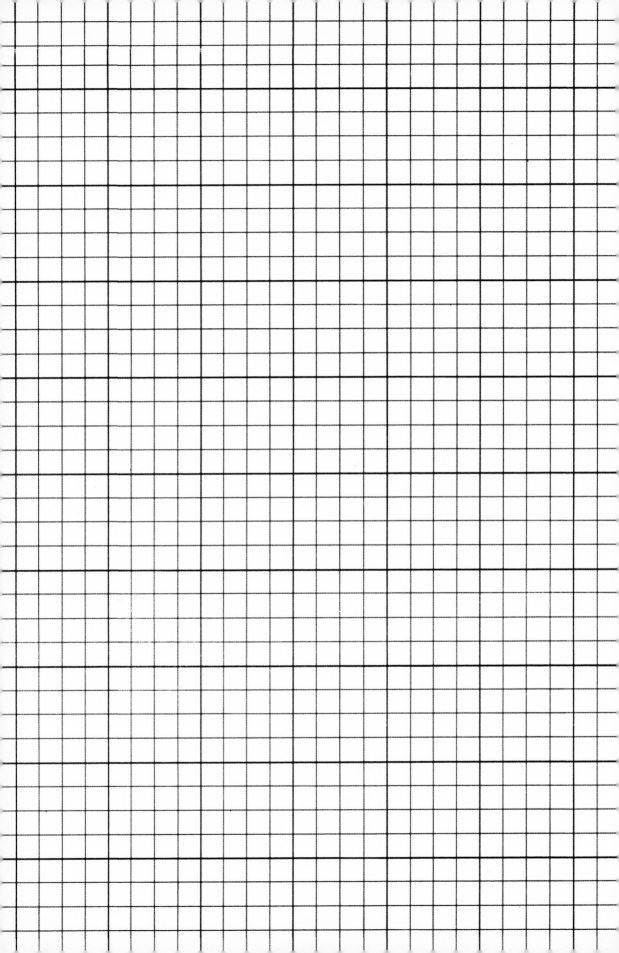

Save time and effort

Measure your room and then draw its outline on the graph paper at the left, letting one square (or ¼ inch) equal one foot. Indicate windows, doors (and which way they swing) electrical outlets, telephone, arched openings, radiators, fireplace, and built-ins. Select the furniture cutouts that are the closest in size to your own pieces and arrange on the graph.

←
¼ inch
equals
one
foot

Dining room

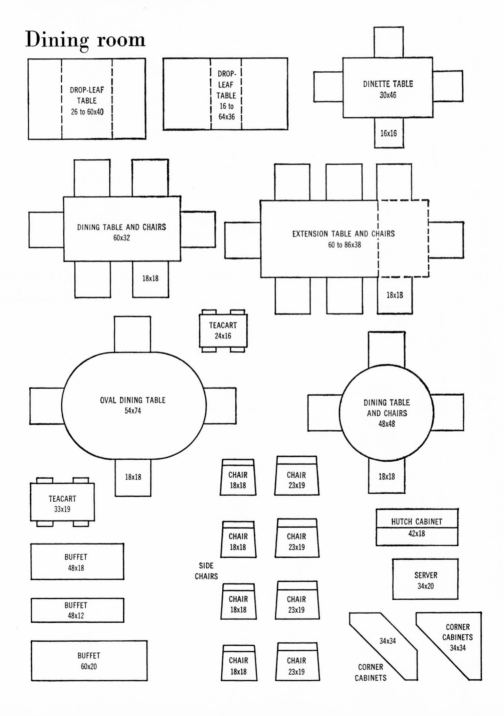

Measure carefully and make your own patterns

The patterns are typical of furniture available today. If they differ 2 or 3 inches from your pieces, it's all right unless you're working in very tight space. If there is a large difference, measure your piece as shown here and then make your own cutout.

Living room

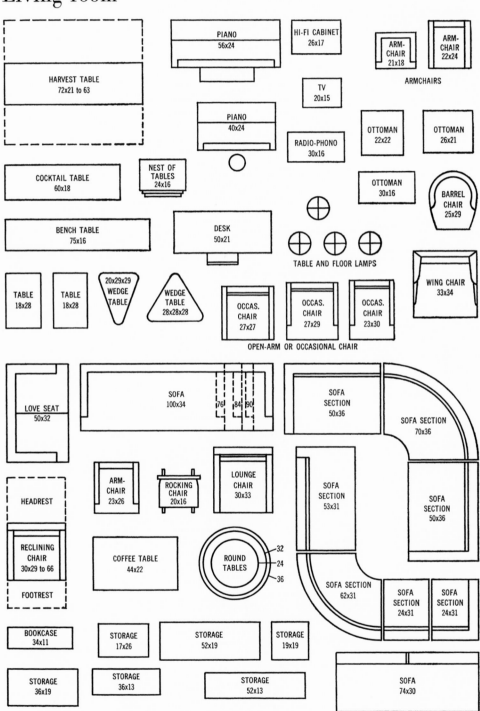

HARVEST TABLE
72x21 to 63

PIANO
56x24

HI-FI CABINET
26x17

ARM-
CHAIR
21x18

ARM-
CHAIR
22x24

ARMCHAIRS

TV
20x15

PIANO
40x24

RADIO-PHONO
30x16

OTTOMAN
22x22

OTTOMAN
26x21

COCKTAIL TABLE
60x18

NEST OF
TABLES
24x16

OTTOMAN
30x16

BARREL
CHAIR
25x29

BENCH TABLE
75x16

DESK
50x21

TABLE AND FLOOR LAMPS

WING CHAIR
33x34

TABLE
18x28

TABLE
18x28

20x29x29
WEDGE
TABLE

WEDGE
TABLE
28x28x28

OCCAS.
CHAIR
27x27

OCCAS.
CHAIR
27x29

OCCAS.
CHAIR
23x30

OPEN-ARM OR OCCASIONAL CHAIR

LOVE SEAT
50x32

SOFA
100x34   76 84 90

SOFA
SECTION
50x36

SOFA SECTION
70x36

HEADREST

ARM-
CHAIR
23x26

ROCKING
CHAIR
20x16

LOUNGE
CHAIR
30x33

SOFA
SECTION
53x31

SOFA
SECTION
50x36

RECLINING
CHAIR
30x29 to 66

FOOTREST

COFFEE TABLE
44x22

ROUND
TABLES

32
24
36

SOFA SECTION
62x31

SOFA
SECTION
24x31

SOFA
SECTION
24x31

BOOKCASE
34x11

STORAGE
17x26

STORAGE
52x19

STORAGE
19x19

STORAGE
36x19

STORAGE
36x13

STORAGE
52x13

SOFA
74x30

Bedroom

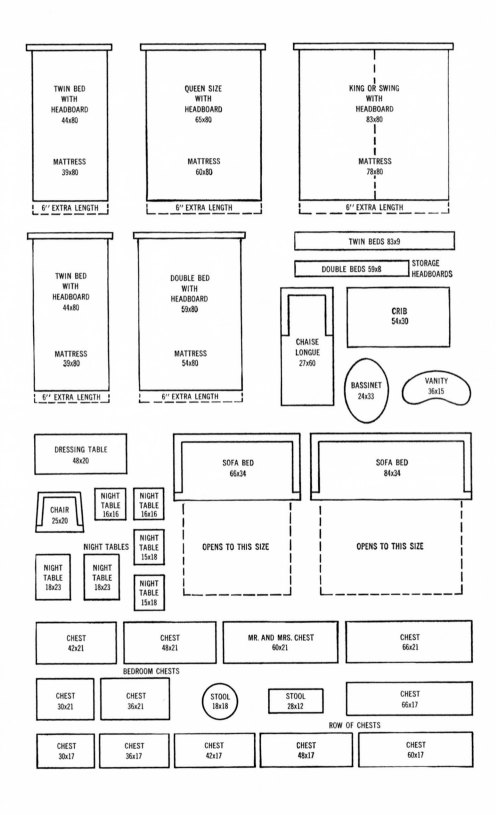

TWIN BED WITH HEADBOARD 44x80

MATTRESS 39x80

6" EXTRA LENGTH

QUEEN SIZE WITH HEADBOARD 65x80

MATTRESS 60x80

6" EXTRA LENGTH

KING OR SWING WITH HEADBOARD 83x80

MATTRESS 78x80

6" EXTRA LENGTH

TWIN BED WITH HEADBOARD 44x80

MATTRESS 39x80

6" EXTRA LENGTH

DOUBLE BED WITH HEADBOARD 59x80

MATTRESS 54x80

6" EXTRA LENGTH

TWIN BEDS 83x9

DOUBLE BEDS 59x8

STORAGE HEADBOARDS

CHAISE LONGUE 27x60

CRIB 54x30

BASSINET 24x33

VANITY 36x15

DRESSING TABLE 48x20

SOFA BED 66x34

SOFA BED 84x34

CHAIR 25x20

NIGHT TABLE 16x16

NIGHT TABLE 16x16

NIGHT TABLE 15x18

NIGHT TABLES

OPENS TO THIS SIZE

OPENS TO THIS SIZE

NIGHT TABLE 18x23

NIGHT TABLE 18x23

NIGHT TABLE 15x18

CHEST 42x21

CHEST 48x21

MR. AND MRS. CHEST 60x21

CHEST 66x21

BEDROOM CHESTS

CHEST 30x21

CHEST 36x21

STOOL 18x18

STOOL 28x12

CHEST 66x17

ROW OF CHESTS

CHEST 30x17

CHEST 36x17

CHEST 42x17

CHEST 48x17

CHEST 60x17

Index

D-E

F

G-H

K

L

Decorator credits

This Better Homes & Gardens Decorating Book illustrates the good taste in decorating of hundreds of homeowners throughout the country. Some of these illustrations also represent the work of some of America's leading professional interior decorators and designers. In salute to these decorators, we have listed their names below and the pages on which you'll find their work.

James Adler, A.I.D., 60
Ada Allen, 84
B. Altman, 47, 188
Shirley Anderson, 286
Joan Baer, 230
Mrs. Terry Bailey, 346
Barclay and Brown, 247
Frederick H. Bernard, Jr., A.I.D., 335
Brown of Black Bros., 46
Everett Brown, A.I.D., 18, 88
Bloomingdale's, 42, 72, 214, 237, 266
Campbell of Levoy Studios, 280
Cannell & Chaffin, 264
Nancy Chase, 78
Agnes Cornell, 238
Bert Curtin, A.I.D., 180
Jack Dawson, 14
Claud d'Avray, A.I.D., 316
Charles E. Day, A.I.D., 11
Decorative Manner, 44, 232, 329
Robert Eichhorn of Manor House, 9
Philip Enfield, 221
Toney Frampton, A.I.D., 350
Blanche Fulkerson, A.I.D., 204
John Garner, 165
Greenwich House, Inc.:
    Walter Farmer, A.I.D., 80;
    Louise S. Roth, 189, 231
Harbine Chatfield, Inc.:
    Edmund Lawyer, A.I.D., 40;
    John Chesteen, A.I.D., 364
Syd Haskell, A.I.D., 73
Marion Heuer Interiors, 10,
    11, 16, 30, 32, 34, 52, 160, 207,
    211, 241, 248, 250, 287, 297
Fredirick Hey, 350
Josephine Heyman, 89, 373
Lucian Horton, 343
Humphrey & Hardenbergh, Inc., 303
Dorothy Jennings, 87
Philip Johnson, 223
Ju-Al Interiors, 83, 183, 201, 303

Pat Klorer, 250
Frederick Kreitzer, 12, 251
Don Lee, 198
Ruth W. Lee, Home Furnishings
    Consultant
Lehmans, 298, 299
Bonnie Lilly, 91
Robert S. Lindenthal, N.S.I.D., 38, 195
Lubliner & Himmel, 27, 64, 79, 81, 93,
    127, 162, 192, 208, 213, 277, 319, 320
Ted Luderowski, 302
Paul MacAlister, 326
Alderman Studios:
    Charles Anna Marsh, A.I.D.,
    108-115, 136-158, 235, 363
Marshall Field & Company, 249
Evelyn Mayer, 199
Bob McLain, L. S. Ayres, 71
Tommi Miller, A.I.D., 269
George Nelson, 95
Sarah Pagoria, 342
C. Donald Popplestone, A.I.D., 161
Marian Quinlan, A.I.D., 305
Warren Ramsey, 240
Ben Rose, 202
Ethel Samuels, 18, 172, 307
Walter Sawicki, A.I.D., 212
Cedo Schwall, 85
Agatha Shoenbrun, A.I.D., 261
Betty Siegel, 163, 200, 276
Martin Sirlin, A.I.D., 133
Lucille Smith, Inc., 182
C. Eugene Stephenson, A.I.D., 222
Stix, Baer & Fuller, 36, 196
Wallace V. Street, 267
Everett Parker Stutts, A.I.D., 191
William A. Taylor, 308, 310
Lucile Ullman, A.I.D., 184
William Votova, 159, 243, 315
William Wachsman, 187, 193
Watson & Boaler, 257
Elizabeth Whitney, A.I.D., 97